# FOOTBALL STARS OF THE '70S

## AND WHERE ARE THEY NOW?

# FOOTBALL STARS OF THE '70S

## AND WHERE ARE THEY NOW?

### Dean P. Hayes

Sutton Publishing Limited
Phoenix Mill · Thrupp · Stroud
Gloucestershire · GL5 2BU

First published 2003

All pictures courtesy of the *Lancashire Evening Post*.

*Title page photograph*: Manchester United
goalkeeper Gary Bailey gathers the ball safely,
watched by Gordon McQueen and Stewart
Houston, while Arsenal striker Alan Sunderland
waits in anticipation.

**British Library Cataloguing in Publication Data**
A catalogue record for this book is available from the
British Library.

ISBN 0-7509-3237-6

Typeset in 10.5/13.5 Photina.
Typesetting and origination by
Sutton Publishing Limited.
Printed and bound in England by
J.H. Haynes & Co. Ltd, Sparkford.

In the 1970s Derby County and Nottingham Forest were two of the best teams in the country,
which only served to increase their traditional rivalry. Here, Gerry Daly is seen beating
Archie Gemmill to the ball.

# Contents

# Introduction

After the dramatic rise in footballing standards in England during the sixties, culminating in England's triumph in the World Cup in 1966 and Manchester United winning the European Cup in 1968, playing standards in the early part of the seventies fell. Players became involved in controversy as standards of behaviour slumped on and off the field. This led to a fall in gates, which only added to the gloom.

Despite this early disappointment, Arsenal kicked off the decade by emulating Tottenham Hotspur's achievement of ten years earlier and winning the League Championship and FA Cup 'double'; but that was the start of a dark period for the Gunners' and they had to wait eighteen years for another title.

Derby County, under Brian Clough, won the League in 1971/72 and they did it again in 1974/75, although by now Dave Mackay was in charge. Leeds United also claimed the crown on one occasion – in 1973/74 – but for much of the seventies the League Championship trophy had a permanent home at Anfield.

Liverpool took the title five times, including three out of the last four years, as they began a period of complete dominance of the English League scene. Bob Paisley had built a fantastic side and it appeared as though one brilliant team just merged into another.

Liverpool were virtually untouchable and the Red machine rolled over everything in its path, both at home and abroad, where they won the European Cup two years in succession: 1977 and 1978. The only time their League dominance was challenged was in 1977/78, when Nottingham Forest upset the apple cart and Liverpool had to settle for second place. And the man who masterminded Forest's takeover was none other than Brian Clough, repeating his achievement with Derby in 1971/72.

And that triumph cannot be overstated: 'Old Big 'Ead' (as he dubbed himself) took two unfashionable clubs to the heights of the English game in his own inimitable style, with teams playing with great flair to win them a place in the nation's favour.

Older fans can be forgiven for assuming they will derive greater pleasure from *Football Stars of the '70s* than today's young supporters – after all they watched these stars week in week out for more than a decade. But hopefully young fans too will enjoy the profiles of yesterday's stars, whose skills and achievements they will have long grown tired of being extolled by their parents and grandparents time and time again!

Included in the information for each player is a table showing the number of games which they played for a team and their goalscoring record. Games in which a player came on as a substitute are shown in brackets. The tables cover league appearances only – not FA Cup, League Cup, or European Cup matches.

*Dean P. Hayes*
*Pembrokeshire, October 2003*

# The Players

# DAVID ARMSTRONG
Midfielder
Born 26.12.54, Durham

**LEAGUE RECORD**

|  | A | G |
|---|---|---|
| Middlesbrough | 357 (2) | 59 |
| Southampton | 222 | 59 |
| Bournemouth | 6 (3) | 2 |

**HONOURS**
Second Division Championship
  1973/74
Anglo-Scottish Cup winners 1976
3 England caps

Midfielder DAVID ARMSTRONG holds an incredible Middlesbrough club record that is unlikely ever to be surpassed. Over a seven-year period, Boro fans never failed to see Armstrong turning out for the club and his record of 356 consecutive League and Cup appearances stands as testimony to his consistency on the left side of the Teeside club's midfield.

Armstrong, who had been with Middlesbrough since he was nine, turned professional on New Year's Day 1971 and made his league debut as a seventeen-year-old against Queens Park Rangers in March 1972.

Within twelve months, Armstrong had established himself as a first-team regular and after missing Boro's trip to Huddersfield Town in March 1973 he started the phenomenal record run of consecutive first-team appearances that only ended when his name was missing from the teamsheet for the visit of Nottingham Forest in September 1980.

Armstrong's displays in the Boro midfield had led to him winning international recognition in the form of England Under-23 and 'B' caps before, in May 1980, Bobby Robson called him into the England side against Australia at Sydney. It was the only occasion he appeared in an England shirt while with Middlesbrough, although he was to win two more caps later.

In October 1980, David Armstrong, then just 25 years old, was awarded a testimonial against Middlesbrough's 1973/74 promotion-winning team. Less than twelve months later, the midfielder who had scored 77 goals in 431 League and Cup games, was sold to Southampton for a fee of £600,000.

He quickly fitted into the Saints' midfield and in 1981/82, his first season at the Dell, he scored fifteen goals, an impressive total in the face of some ultra-defensive football.

Although naturally a left-sided player, his reading of the game allowed him to play in a variety of positions. He was an obvious choice as the club's captain and his talents earned him further caps against West Germany and Wales while at the Dell. He had appeared in 262 League and Cup games for the club when contractual disputes led to him leaving the Dell and joining Bournemouth, where he ended his first-class career.

David Armstrong still lives on the south coast and is a commentator on local radio covering Southampton's matches. Prior to that he was in charge of commercial operations at Waterlooville FC, having previously worked for Hampshire Schools as a sports liaison officer and for Reading as an officer for Football in the Community.

# PETER BARNES
Winger
Born 10.6.57, Manchester

The son of Ken Barnes, the former Manchester City wing-half and chief scout, PETER BARNES made many dazzling displays for the Maine Road club, earning himself nine Under-21 caps, and in the 1976 League Cup Final, he scored in City's 2–1 win over Newcastle United. He ended the season being named 'Young Player of the Year'.

In November 1977 he won the first of twenty-two full caps for England when he played against Italy in a World Cup qualifier. An exciting winger who was able to beat his opponents with ease, he was surprisingly allowed to leave Maine Road and join West Bromwich Albion for a fee of £650,000 in 1979.

He ended his first season at the Hawthorns as the club's leading scorer with fifteen goals and netted another ten the following season before being sold to Leeds United for £930,000.

He never reproduced the form he showed at Manchester City and was soon loaned out to Spanish club Real Betis on a £130,000 option for one year. Twelve months later he was back at Leeds, who were now a Second Division club. When he joined the Yorkshire club, he was one of their most expensive players, but in October 1984 he left to join Coventry City for just £65,000, this after a brief loan spell with Manchester United.

He spent a season at Highfield Road before returning to Old Trafford on a permanent basis. He later rejoined Manchester City before loan spells with Bolton and Port Vale were followed by a free transfer to Hull City. In November 1988 he had one game for Portuguese club Farense before joining Bolton Wanderers. His stay at Burnden Park lasted a month before he moved to Sunderland.

He then played in Ireland with Drogheda on a match-to-match basis before trying his luck in the NASL with Tampa Bay Rowdies. There followed spells with a number of non-League clubs including Northwich Victoria, Radcliffe Borough and Mossley after which he managed Runcorn.

Since then he has worked as a summariser for radio stations in the north-west, helped run the Manchester City social club at Maine Road, and coached youngsters at City's Platt Lane training complex.

## KEVIN BEATTIE
Central Defender
Born 18.12.53, Carlisle

A product of the Ipswich Town youth policy masterminded by Bobby Robson, KEVIN BEATTIE made his league debut for the club on the opening day of the 1972/73 season in a 2–1 victory over Manchester United at Old Trafford.

Two weeks later Ipswich travelled to Leeds United, where Beattie scored his first league goal in an exciting 3–3 draw. The Portman Road club ended the 1972/73 season in fourth place, their best showing since they won the League Championship eleven years earlier. Beattie had played in all but a handful of games at the heart of the defence – he was by now one of the game's greatest creative forces and a huge favourite with the Ipswich crowd. Early in the next season, Beattie performed outstandingly, in an Ipswich side that hovered in mid-table before ending the season again in fourth place. He and captain Mick Mills were ever-present in the team, and Beattie so impressed his fellow professionals that they elected him as the first PFA 'Young Player of the Year', an award presented to him by Leeds United manager Don Revie.

In the following season, Revie succeeded Joe Mercer as England manager and in his fourth match in charge selected Beattie as the centre of England's defence for their European Championship qualifier against Cyprus at Wembley. England won 5–0, with Malcolm Macdonald creating a postwar record by scoring all England's goals. The Ipswich player almost got his name on the scoresheet, but in the process of scoring he was adjudged to have fouled the goalkeeper. He went on to win nine caps for his country, all but one under Revie's management.

In 1978, Beattie played in the Ipswich team that beat Arsenal in the FA Cup Final. He could have become one of the all-time great players but he had to undergo five operations on his right knee in four years. After scoring 32 goals in 307 first-team games, he played briefly for Colchester United and Middlesbrough before the injury brought his league career to a premature end in 1982.

He played briefly in Sweden and then became player-coach to Kongsberg in Norway before returning to England to run a pub. Illness prevented him from pursuing this career but he now provides coaching on a part-time basis for Carlisle United. He also writes a weekly column in the *Evening Star*, Ipswich's local paper, and attends most matches at Portman Road.

**LEAGUE RECORD**

| | A | G |
|---|---|---|
| Sheffield United | 106 (1) | 31 |
| Chelsea | 74 (1) | 20 |
| Crystal Palace | 41 | 11 |
| Leicester City | 156 (7) | 12 |
| Notts County | 33 | 0 |
| Blackburn Rovers | 17 (1) | 0 |
| Luton Town | 9 (1) | 0 |
| Hereford United | 11 | 0 |

# ALAN BIRCHENALL
## Midfielder
### Born 22.8.45, East Ham

ALAN BIRCHENALL started his playing career as an extrovert blond striker, gaining four England Under-23 caps while figuring as a skilful foil for Mick Jones at Sheffield United. In November 1967 he became Chelsea manager Dave Sexton's first signing, when the Stamford Bridge boss paid £100,000 for his services.

He was a stylist who delighted in receiving the ball with his back to goal and spreading it wide with his cultured left foot, but his instinctive tendency to drop back into midfield meant that he was not the ideal partner for Peter Osgood, who was in this respect a similar player. Birchenall's effectiveness in the air and persistent running made him hugely popular with the Chelsea fans, despite his indifferent goal-scoring record. However, just after he had netted two goals in the London derby win over Arsenal and clinched the Blues' victory in a third round League Cup replay against Leeds United, a knee injury in a match against West Bromwich Albion sidelined him for three months.

While he was out of action, Ian Hutchison and Peter Osgood struck up a spectacular double act; when this was followed by the signing of Keith Weller, Birchenall realised he had no future with Chelsea and joined Crystal Palace.

His stay at Selhurst Park was brief and in September 1971 he joined Leicester City. At Filbert Street he assumed a deeper-lying schemer's role as attack-orientated City's fortunes ebbed and flowed entertainingly in the early '70s. While with the Foxes he had a loan spell with Notts County before trying his luck in the NASL with San Jose Earthquakes and Memphis Rogues. On his return to this country, he had brief spells in the lower divisions with Blackburn Rovers, Luton Town and Hereford United.

Birchenall then became player-manager of Trowbridge before returning to Filbert Street as Leicester's press officer. In recent years his commercial interests have included running the Griffin pub in Swithland and running a ladies footwear import business. He also helps charities with his team of former Leicester City favourites, known as the Geriatric Megastars.

# STUART BOAM
Central Defender
Born 28.1.48, Kirkby-in-Ashfield

**LEAGUE RECORD**

|  | A | G |
|---|---|---|
| Mansfield Town | 186 (4) | 4 |
| Middlesbrough | 322 | 14 |
| Newcastle United | 69 | 1 |
| Hartlepool United | 1 | 0 |

**HONOURS**
Division Two Championship 1973/74
Anglo-Scottish Cup 1975/76

A centre-half in every traditional sense, STUART BOAM began his career with his local club, Mansfield Town, going on to make 170 appearances for the Stags before joining Middlesbrough for a fee of £50,000 in May 1971.

Boam captained Middlesbrough throughout the 1970s, one of the north-east club's most successful decades, first under Stan Anderson, then Jack Charlton, and finally John Neal. He was the rock on which the Boro defence was built.

He developed a formidable central defensive partnership with Willie Maddren and though the Nottinghamshire-born defender never received as much media attention as his colleague, he was still adored by Boro fans. In fact, a favourite chant of Ayresome Park's Holgate End was 'Six feet two, eyes of blue, big Stuart Boam is after you!' Boam skippered Middlesbrough to the Second Division Championship in 1973/74, with the defence being the cornerstone of the side. Boam and Maddren were the perfect foils for each other as the side adapted to life in the top flight.

Though Boam led Boro to success in the Anglo-Scottish Cup in 1975/76, it was a great disappointment that he didn't skipper the side to a major honour. When Jack Charlton left Ayresome Park, Boam had a run-in with the club's new manager John Neal, which resulted in him losing the captaincy for a brief period. However, Neal soon realised that Stuart Boam was the leader in the dressing-room and restored him to the role of skipper.

Despite this, on the eve of the 1979/80 season, Boam left the club in a shock move to Second Division rivals Newcastle United for a fee of £100,000. Boam, who was now thirty-one, had appeared in 393 League and Cup games for Boro. After Boam arrived at St James Park, he helped to give a shaky Magpies side back-four experience and stability for two seasons in their bid to climb out of Division Two.

In July 1981, Boam returned to Mansfield Town as the Field Mill club's player-manager, before having further spells as a player with Hartlepool United and non-League Guisborough Town.

On ending his involvement with the game, he returned to his home town of Kirkby-in-Ashfield near Mansfield and was employed as a manager of Kodak Photographic Company.

## STAN BOWLES
### Midfielder
### Born 24.12.48, Manchester

**LEAGUE CAREER**

| | A | G |
|---|---|---|
| Manchester City | 15 (2) | 2 |
| Bury | 5 | 0 |
| Crewe Alexandra | 51 | 18 |
| Carlisle United | 33 | 12 |
| Queens Park Rangers | 255 | 70 |
| Nottingham Forest | 19 | 2 |
| Leyton Orient | 46 | 7 |
| Brentford | 80 (1) | 16 |

**HONOURS**
5 England caps

One of the game's most colourful characters, STAN BOWLES was a player who never realised his full potential during his early days in the game. Having started out promisingly with Manchester City, he disappeared from the big-time for nearly three years, playing for Bury, Crewe Alexandra and Carlisle United.

When Bowles signed for Queens Park Rangers in September 1972, some said it was a high-risk expense at £112,000. How wrong they were, for Stan Bowles was probably the finest player to appear for the club.

As the great Rangers side of the mid-1970s grew, built around quality players like Francis, Parkes, McLintock, Thomas and Webb, so did the reputation of Stan Bowles. His ability to improve his game and adapt his genius was a revelation. With his flair and ability, it was natural that he would eventually be selected by England, although he was capped only five times. Stan Bowles was an entertainer with a great left foot; he had good tight control, good dribbling skills and he liked to chip and curl his shots at the goal.

Bowles had scored 97 goals in 315 League and Cup games for Rangers when in December 1979 Brian Clough paid £250,000 to take him to Nottingham Forest. He was only at the City Ground for a few months, however, appearing in nineteen games before moving on to Orient. He ended his first-class career at Brentford, yet for a player who provided so much entertainment, he left the game with so little.

Bowles often got into the headlines for all the wrong reasons – he was a gambler, and every now and then his liking for a bet would introduce a fresh crisis into his life. In 1987 his domestic life was in turmoil but Brentford staged a testimonial for him – the committee investing the proceeds of the game in a trust to ensure that Stan had a regular income.

Unemployed for a long time after hanging up his boots, he did have a spell helping out with the coaching at Brentford when invited to do so by the then Bees' manager David Webb. Nowadays, he can be found in the hospitality suite at Loftus Road, helping out on Queens Park Rangers match days.

# LIAM BRADY

Midfielder
Born 13.2.56, Dublin

## LEAGUE CAREER

|  | A | G |
| --- | --- | --- |
| Arsenal | 227 (8) | 43 |
| West Ham United | 79 (10) | 8 |

**HONOURS**
FA Cup 1978/79
Italian League 1980/81, 1981/82
72 Republic of Ireland caps

Without doubt, LIAM BRADY must rank as one of the greatest players ever to pull on the famous red and white shirt of Arsenal. The outstanding player of his generation, he was the most creative of midfielders with a highly educated left foot. He could pass over any distance, take on markers and leave them for dead, and lash spectacular goals from long distance. A player of the highest order, his vision and imagination touched heights most players only dream of.

When Arsenal boss Terry Neill sold Alan Ball to Southampton in December 1976, Brady, who had made his Gunners debut in October 1973, became the club's midfield general, and in seven seasons as a Gunner he scored 59 goals in 307 League and Cup games.

His outstanding display in the 1979 FA Cup Final earned Brady the only winner's medal of his Arsenal career. He was the general who plotted Manchester United's downfall in that final. Arsenal somehow managed to lose a two-goal cushion in the dying minutes of the tie, only to snatch the game with a Brady-inspired winner in the last seconds to run out 3–2 winners.

Brady collected runners-up medals in the same competition either side of the 1979 success. He wasn't fully fit in 1978 when he was substituted in the Gunners' 1–0 defeat by Ipswich Town. Arsenal also lost the 1980 final 1–0, this time to West Ham. His final 'big game' for Arsenal was the 1980 European Cup Winners' Cup Final against Valencia, which they lost on penalties to the Spanish club.

During the summer months, Brady turned down Manchester United's £1.5 million bid and moved to Italian giants Juventus for £600,000. Few foreign players could have settled into Italian football so quickly and in each of his two seasons with the club, Juventus won the Italian League Championship. On the arrival of Michel Platini, Brady moved to Sampdoria in a £1.75 million deal before ending seven years in Italian football with Ascoli.

On his return to England he joined West Ham United, and it wasn't long before he was showing that he hadn't lost any of the skills which had made him a superstar at Arsenal. However, Brady, who had made seventy-two appearances for the Republic of Ireland, announced his retirement at the end of the 1987/88 season.

In June 1991 he became the first manager of Celtic who had not played for the Glasgow giants. Though he brought his own style of free-flowing football to

Parkhead, he resigned in October 1993 after a string of poor results. In January 1994 he was appointed manager of Brighton but resigned just under two years later to return to Highbury as head of Arsenal's youth development programme.

# TREVOR BROOKING

Midfielder
Born 2.10.48, Barking

**LEAGUE RECORD**

| | A | G |
|---|---|---|
| West Ham United | 521 (7) | 88 |

**HONOURS**
FA Cup 1974/75, 1979/80
Second Division Championship
  1980/81
47 England caps

One of the greatest players ever to wear the claret and blue of West Ham United, TREVOR BROOKING was 'a rare and refined talent that only comes along once every decade'.

Born in Barking, he grew up a West Ham supporter and joined the club straight from Ilford County High School in 1965. He made his first appearance for the Hammers in a 3–3 draw at Burnley in August 1967, though he took his time to establish himself in the first team, initially as a centre-forward! Following the transfer of Martin Peters to Spurs in March 1970, Brooking settled down as a left-sided midfield player, though when Ron Greenwood left him out of the side midway through the following season, he went on the transfer list.

**FACT**

On 6 January 1975, Bobby Gould was playing for West Ham United at Southampton in an FA Cup third round tie. He was taken off at half-time when it was discovered that he had played for over half an hour with a broken leg but had managed to head a goal. West Ham won 2–1.

Capped once at Under-23 level, Trevor Brooking went on to win forty-seven full caps after making his international debut in a 2–2 draw against Argentina at Wembley in 1974. Perhaps the international game that gave him the greatest pleasure was the World Cup qualifying game in Hungary in 1981 when his two goals helped England to a 3–1 win and a place in the finals.

First voted 'Hammer of the Year' in 1971, he is the only player to win the award in three consecutive seasons, 1975–1977. He won two FA Cup winners' medals and on the second occasion, in 1980, it was Brooking who scored the only goal of the game when he stooped low to guide Stuart Pearson's shot past Pat Jennings and into the Arsenal net. He also won runners-up medals in the 1976 European Cup Winners' Cup Final and the League Cup Final of 1981. In 1980/81 he won a Second Division Championship medal, when he was probably at his peak of his form.

Also in 1981 he was awarded the MBE, an admirable reward for his loyalty to West Ham United. He had played in 635 first-team games for the Hammers, scoring 102 goals, when he finally decided to quit at the end of the 1983/84 season. There is no doubt that he could have gone on playing for another couple of seasons at least, but he wanted to leave at the top.

In 1989 he was appointed to the Sports Council as the representative of regional chairmen. Now, while also running Colbrook Plastics Ltd, a plastic-binding company based in the East End of London, he is a succinct and shrewd match summariser for BBC radio and television. Trevor Brooking was a true sportsman, one of football's gentlemen at a time when the game was becoming increasingly aggressive.

# TONY BROWN

Midfielder
Born 3.10.45, Oldham

**LEAGUE RECORD**

|  | A | G |
| --- | --- | --- |
| West Bromwich Albion | 561 (13) | 218 |
| Torquay United | 38 (7) | 11 |

**HONOURS**
League Cup 1965/66
1 England cap

TONY BROWN holds the West Bromwich Albion club records for most League appearances (574) and most goals (218) in a twenty-year career at the Hawthorns.

Originally a goal-scoring wing-half, netting on his debut against Ipswich Town in September 1963, after a couple of seasons Brown established himself as a versatile first-team regular in the Albion side, playing in all the midfield and forward positions at the club as well as taking the penalties. He missed very few of the sixty or so spot-kicks he attempted.

He was a first choice at the Hawthorns from 1965 to 1979, topping the club's scoring charts time after time. In 1970/71 his twenty-eight goals made him the First Division's top scorer and helped him win his only full international cap when he played for England against Malta, although he did represent Young England and the Football League.

When the more defence-minded Don Howe took over as manager, Brown's goal-scoring rate declined slightly. However, when Ron Atkinson took charge in January 1978, Brown gained a new lease of life, ending his last season as the club's top scorer with twenty-three goals. In 1978/79, when Albion finished runners-up to Liverpool in the First Division, Brown still weighed in with fourteen valuable goals.

Perhaps his most spectacular goal came in the 2–1 FA Cup defeat at Sheffield Wednesday, when he volleyed the ball from over his shoulder past England keeper Ron Springett, though his best remembered strike was the goal against his home-town team Oldham Athletic, which gained Albion promotion to the First Division in 1976.

Brown played the last of nearly 900 senior appearances for the club in 1980, moving to end his first-class career with Torquay United in October 1981, after the arrival of Albion's new manager Ronnie Allen. In 1984 Tony Brown returned to the Hawthorns as a coach after the appointment of Johnny Giles as manager but left after Giles's resignation in October 1985, to take up a post as assistant manager to former Albion team-mate Gary Pendrey at Birmingham City.

Tony Brown, who was granted a second testimonial in 1997, nearly twenty-three years after the first, has had hip operations during the past few years, but still manages to keep in touch with the game by attending all of his beloved West Bromwich Albion's home games.

# GEORGE BURLEY
## Right-Back
### Born 3.6.56, Cumnock

**LEAGUE RECORD**

|  | A | G |
|---|---|---|
| Ipswich Town | 394 | 6 |
| Sunderland | 54 | 0 |
| Gillingham | 46 | 2 |
| Colchester United | 5 (2) | 0 |

**HONOURS**
FA Cup 1977/78
11 Scotland caps

An adventurous defender, GEORGE BURLEY joined Ipswich Town straight from school and made a memorable debut for the Suffolk club at the age of seventeen years and 209 days, when he completely marked George Best out of the game in a 2–0 defeat against Manchester United at Old Trafford on 29 December 1973.

Over the next twelve seasons, Burley missed very few games and in 1975/76, when the club finished sixth in Division One, he was ever present. In 1976/77 he was voted the club's 'Player of the Year' and in 1978 he won an FA Cup winners' medal when a Roger Osborne goal was enough to beat Arsenal in the Wembley final. Burley, who had won international honours for Scotland at schoolboy and Under-21 level, won the first of eleven full caps for his country in 1979 when he played against Wales.

Sadly he was not a member of the Ipswich side that beat AZ67 Alkmaar to win the UEFA Cup in 1980/81, having severely damaged his knee ligaments in an FA Cup tie at Shrewsbury.

Burley went on to appear in exactly 500 first-team games for Ipswich Town before leaving Portman Road in September 1985 to join Sunderland. He played in 54 league games for the Wearsiders before ending his playing career – or so he thought – with Gillingham.

After spells as manager of Ayr United and coach of Motherwell, he took charge at Colchester United, but in December 1994 his career came full circle when he returned to Ipswich as manager. At the time of his appointment, the club were firmly rooted at the foot of the Premier League, and though they beat Leicester City 4–1 and won at Anfield for the very first time, the Blues were relegated. After leading the club to seventh in Division One in 1995/96, Burley took the Blues to the play-offs for the next four seasons, eventually winning promotion in 1999/2000.

In their first season back, Ipswich under Burley finished fifth and so qualified for the following season's UEFA Cup. However, the club were then relegated and after a poor start to the 2002/03 season, Burley was replaced by Joe Royle.

Though his name had been mentioned as a possible contender for the forthcoming managerial vacancy at Fulham, Burley has recently been appointed temporary manager of strife-torn Derby County.

George Burley made 394 league appearances for Ipswich Town.

# KENNY BURNS
### Central Defender
### Born 23.9.53, Glasgow

**LEAGUE RECORD**

|  | A | G |
| --- | --- | --- |
| Birmingham City | 163 (7) | 45 |
| Nottingham Forest | 137 | 13 |
| Leeds United | 54 (2) | 2 |
| Derby County | 36 (2) | 2 |
| Notts County | 2 | 0 |
| Barnsley | 19 (2) | 0 |

**HONOURS**

League Champions 1977/78
League Cup 1977/78, 1978/79
European Cup 1978/79, 1979/80
European Super Cup 1979/80
20 Scotland caps

Though he began his career with Glasgow Rangers, it was with Birmingham City that KENNY BURNS first came to prominence. He joined the St Andrew's club as an apprentice in the summer of 1970 and signed professional forms the following year. He made his League debut as a substitute at Hull City in September 1971, though it was 1973/74 before he established himself as a first-team regular at St Andrew's. During that season, Burns, who had won Scottish youth and Under-23 honours, won the first of his twenty full caps when he played against West Germany. In that 1973/74 campaign, Burns netted his first hat-trick in League football as the Blues drew 3–3 at Leicester City. In 1976/77, his last season with Birmingham, he formed a formidable striking partnership with Trevor Francis and scored nineteen goals in thirty-six games, including four in a 5–1 home win over Derby County. Though he had more than his fair share of disciplinary problems, he had scored fifty-three goals in 204 games for the Blues when Brian Clough signed him for Nottingham Forest for a fee of £150,000 in the summer of 1977.

> **FACT**
>
> Nottingham Forest secured promotion to the First Division in 1977 thanks to an own goal from Millwall's Jon Moore. Later that evening, Forest supporters voted Moore their 'Player of the Year'!

Switched to the centre of defence, Burns was outstanding as Forest won the League Championship and League Cup in his first season at the City Ground. He was selected as the Football Writers' Association 'Player of the Year' and went to Argentina with the Scotland World Cup squad.

The popular Scotsman went on to win two European Cup winners' medals with Forest but in October 1981 a lucrative contract lured him to Leeds United.

At Elland Road, Burns was also used in midfield but he couldn't stop United sliding into Division Two. He was loaned to Derby County in March 1983 and signed permanently for the Rams in February 1984. A year later he went on loan to Notts County and moved to Barnsley in August 1985.

On leaving the first-class scene, he joined former Forest colleague John Robertson at Sutton Town and in the summer of 1986 had trials with Swedish

club IF Elfsborg. After a period as manager of Sutton Town, he joined Stafford Rangers before having spells with Gainsborough Trinity and Grantham.

He later ran a pub in Marchington near Uttoxeter and can nowadays be seen back at the City Ground, hosting the occasional Match Day, as well as writing a column for the *Nottingham Evening Post*.

## LEAGUE RECORD

|  | A | G |
|---|---|---|
| Coventry City | 245 (7) | 33 |
| Wolves | 231 (6) | 21 |
| Millwall | 8 | 1 |

## HONOURS
League Cup 1979/80
Second Division Champions
  1976/77
6 Scotland caps

# WILLIE CARR
## Midfielder
### Born 6.1.50, Glasgow

A slightly built but highly effective midfield grafter, who worked tirelessly behind his strikers, red-haired WILLIE CARR had natural football ability in spades. His excellent touch and foresight, plus a capacity for hard work, made him a player who simply couldn't be left out of the team.

Though born in Glasgow, Carr moved to Cambridge with his parents at the age of thirteen and was actually chosen for an England schoolboy trial.

After joining Coventry City, he graduated through the ranks, first featuring in a star-studded Sky Blues youth side before eventually winning a first-team place against Arsenal in September 1967. By the start of the 1968/69 season, Carr was an established member of the Coventry City side and, although not a prolific scorer, he netted a hat-trick in a 3–0 home win over West Bromwich Albion in August 1969.

Although goals were not Willie Carr's forte, he was famous for his part in the 'donkey-kick' free kick that was introduced to *Match of the Day* viewers in the autumn of 1970.

His performances in midfield led to him winning the first of six full caps for Scotland when he played against Northern Ireland in 1970. Carr seemed certain to be chosen for Scotland's 1974 World Cup squad but unfortunately he badly injured his knee in a clash with Liverpool's Phil Boersma at Highfield Road. Forced to miss the remainder of that 1973/74 campaign, he returned to the Sky Blues side the following season but was obviously struggling. After scoring 37 goals in 298 games he was allowed to join Wolverhampton Wanderers for the knock-down price of £80,000.

At the end of his first season at Molineux, Wolves were relegated – but after winning the Second Division Championship in 1976/77, they entered a purple patch in the club's history, reaching the FA Cup semi-final twice and winning the League Cup in the next three years. Carr had made 289 appearances for Wolves when in August 1982 he joined Millwall. His stay at the Den was brief and he moved into non-League football with Worcester City, later playing for Willenhall and Stourbridge.

Since ending his involvement with the game, Willie Carr has been a salesman selling nuts and bolts for the same company for almost twenty years.

# JIMMY CASE
Midfielder
Born 18.5.54, Liverpool

**LEAGUE RECORD**

|  | A | G |
|---|---|---|
| Liverpool | 170 (16) | 23 |
| Brighton & Hove Albion | 154 (5) | 10 |
| Southampton | 213 (2) | 10 |
| Bournemouth | 38 (2) | 1 |
| Halifax Town | 17 (4) | 2 |
| Wrexham | 1 (3) | 0 |
| Darlington | 1 | 0 |

**HONOURS**
League Champions 1975/76, 1976/77,
 1978/79, 1979/80
European Cup 1976/77, 1977/78, 1980/81
UEFA Cup 1975/76
European Super Cup 1977

JIMMY CASE was plucked from local football, signing for Liverpool from non-League South Liverpool in 1973. But he had to wait almost two years before making his League debut – against Queens Park Rangers in April 1975, in an attacking role wide on the right. However, it was midway through the 1975/76 season before Case's explosive talents earned him a regular spot in the Liverpool side at the expense of Brian Hall.

Though not a prolific scorer, he netted a stunning hat-trick in a 3–0 win over Slask Wroclaw of Poland, in a UEFA Cup game played in 15 degrees of frost. The Reds went on to reach the final, where their opponents were FC Bruges. Case had been left out of the first leg at Anfield, but with the Reds two down, he came on as substitute for John Toshack. A series of rampaging runs down the right flank unsettled the previously calm Belgians, as Case inspired a typical Anfield comeback – the Reds winning 3–2, with Jimmy netting the equaliser himself. As if that wasn't sufficient, he ended his first full season with both League Championship and UEFA Cup winners' medals.

In 1976/77, Case found himself in competition with Terry McDermott for one of the midfield positions, but as the Reds' treble-hunting campaign drew to a close, it was Case who wore the number 8 shirt. He played an enterprising part in the club's League and European Cup triumphs, and was the Reds' best player in the FA Cup Final against Manchester United, scoring Liverpool's goal in a 2–1 defeat.

Capped by England at Under-23 level, he never represented his country at senior level but what he missed in international football he more than made up for with a clutch of other honours – three European Cup medals, four League Championship medals and a UEFA Cup medal.

During the 1980/81 season Case lost his place to Sammy Lee, and at the end of the campaign he signed for Brighton and Hove Albion for £350,000. During his second season with the Seagulls, he had the huge satisfaction of returning to Anfield to score the goal that knocked his former team-mates out of the FA Cup. Brighton went on to reach the final but went down 4–0 to Manchester United after the first game had ended all square at 2–2.

Case later moved down the coast to Southampton, as a replacement for Steve Williams, before joining Bournemouth. He later had spells with Halifax Town, Wrexham and Darlington, before returning to Brighton for an ill-fated spell as the club's player-manager. He then continued his managerial apprenticeship, taking over the reins at Dr Marten's League side, Bashley.

# MICK CHANNON
Forward
Born 28.11.48, Orcheston

**LEAGUE RECORD**

|  | A | G |
|---|---|---|
| Southampton | 507 (4) | 185 |
| Manchester City | 71 (1) | 24 |
| Newcastle United | 4 | 1 |
| Bristol Rovers | 4 (5) | 0 |
| Norwich City | 84 (4) | 16 |
| Portsmouth | 34 | 6 |

**HONOURS**
FA Cup 1975/76
League Cup 1984/85
46 England caps

One of the greatest forwards ever to play for Southampton, MICK CHANNON has scored more goals for the club than any other Saints' player.

He scored on his League debut against Bristol City in April 1966, but the following season – Southampton's first season in the top flight – he made just one appearance. However, following the transfer of Martin Chivers, Channon became a first-team regular in 1968/69, going on to become the club's top scorer in 1969/70, when he also won the first of his nine England Under-23 caps.

Channon was Southampton's leading goal-scorer for the next six seasons, with a best of twenty-one in 1973/74. The following season he netted twenty league goals, including hat-tricks against Oxford United and Bristol Rovers – plus another treble in a 5–0 League Cup defeat of Derby County. In 1975/76 he again scored twenty league goals, hitting a hat-trick in the 4–0 local derby defeat of Portsmouth. This was the season that Southampton won the FA Cup, beating Manchester United 1–0 in the final. Channon was a key member of the Saints' side and scored a hat-trick in a 4–0 fifth-round replay win over West Bromwich Albion. Channon's last hat-trick for the club came the following season against Blackpool. His goal-scoring feats also brought him full international honours, scoring twenty goals for England in forty-six appearances.

Sensing he had achieved all he could as a Southampton player, he asked for a transfer, and in the summer of 1977 he joined Manchester City. After two fairly disappointing seasons at Maine Road, Lawrie McMenemy brought him back to the Dell, but in the summer of 1982, Channon parted company with the club for a second time, having scored 215 goals in 580 League and Cup games.

He then had brief spells with Newcastle United and Bristol Rovers before joining Norwich City. He gave the Canaries three years' excellent service and helped them win the Milk Cup in 1985. He later returned to the south coast to play for Portsmouth, before seeing out his career with Finn Harps.

Mick Channon is now a celebrated racehorse trainer based at West Ilseley in Berkshire. Fans who were privileged to see him play can fondly remember each goal being celebrated with his unique windmilling-arm salute!

## LEAGUE RECORD

|  | A | G |
|---|---|---|
| Huddersfield Town | 185 (3) | 12 |
| Leeds United | 394 (6) | 24 |
| Bradford City | 92 | 0 |

## HONOURS
Second Division Champions 1969/70
League Champions 1973/74
27 England caps

# TREVOR CHERRY
Defender
Born 23.2.48, Huddersfield

Beginning his career with his home-town team Huddersfield Town, TREVOR CHERRY played alongside Roy Ellam, mainly in the centre of the Terriers' defence. He captained them to the Second Division Championship in 1969/70 but two seasons later, Town had lost their top-flight status. This was when Leeds United manager Don Revie made a surprise double swoop, taking Cherry and Ellam to Elland Road for £100,000 and £30,000 respectively.

He quickly settled into the full-back berth vacated by the injured Terry Cooper but in subsequent years he operated in a variety of defensive positions and sometimes even in midfield. In only his second season with Leeds, he won a League Championship medal and also won runners-up medals in both the FA Cup and the European Cup Winners Cup.

Cherry, who won twenty-seven full caps for England, is one of the few players to be sent off while playing for his country. It happened in the match against Argentina in Buenos Aires in June 1977, when he lost two front teeth after being punched by an Argentinian player.

He was voted his club's 'Player of the Year' in 1981, but in December 1982, after scoring 32 goals in 485 League and Cup games, he left Leeds to become player-manager of Bradford City.

Cherry steered the Bantams through traumatic times including a receivership and the disastrous fire which claimed fifty-six lives at Valley Parade. City also won the Third Division Championship in that 1984/85 season, earning Cherry the Bells Manager of the Season award for the Division, following his monthly award in November 1984. The fire meant that the club led a nomadic existence over the next year and a half while their home was rebuilt, yet only ten days after the club's emotional return to Valley Parade, Cherry was sacked.

Since then he has been a director of a sports-promotions firm called SLP Consulting, while also doing some local-radio sports work. He once ran his own waste-paper-collection business but is now a director of his first club, Huddersfield Town.

Trevor Cherry won twenty-seven caps for England, and was voted Leeds United
'Player of the Year' in 1981.

## LEAGUE RECORD

| | A | G |
|---|---|---|
| Southampton | 174 (1) | 97 |
| Tottenham Hotspur | 268 (10) | 118 |
| Norwich City | 11 | 4 |
| Brighton & Hove Albion | 4 (1) | 1 |

### HONOURS
League Cup 1970/71, 1972/73
UEFA Cup 1971/72
24 England caps

# MARTIN CHIVERS
## Forward
### Born 27.4.45, Southampton

A big strong forward, MARTIN CHIVERS began his career with his home-town club, Southampton, in the Saints' promotion-winning season of 1965/66. During that campaign, Chivers scored thirty goals in his first twenty-nine outings, including four in a 9–3 win at Wolverhampton Wanderers and a hat-trick as Cardiff City were beaten 5–3 , and played a huge part in the club reaching Division One for the first time.

Chivers eventually became restless at the Dell and in January 1968, after scoring 107 goals in 189 games for the Saints, he joined Spurs, who paid a record £125,000 for his services. He began to repay the fee immediately by scoring at Sheffield Wednesday and then netting both goals in his second outing, a 2–2 draw against Manchester United in the FA Cup third round. He soon gained a further five England Under-23 caps, taking his collection to a record seventeen caps.

He was settling into the Spurs style when he suffered a serious left-knee injury and missed most of the 1968/69 season. On his return, struggling to regain form and confidence, he was dropped, but Bill Nicholson persevered with him. After Jimmy Greaves's departure, Chivers increased his aggression and sense of responsibility, beginning to find the net again with a real vengeance in 1970/71. He scored both Spurs' goals in the 1971 League Cup Final victory over Aston Villa and won the first of his twenty-four England caps, against Malta.

A member of the Spurs UEFA Cup-winning team of 1972 (he sealed the Final first-leg victory over Wolves with two brilliant strikes) and the League Cup-winning side of 1973, Chivers also played in both legs of the 1974 UEFA Cup Final against Feyenoord.

In July 1976, Chivers, who had scored 174 goals in 367 games, left White Hart Lane to join Swiss club Servette, returning to England two years later to play for Norwich City and then Brighton and Hove Albion. However, eventually finding that he was no longer up to the demands of League football, he tried his hand at management, with Vard of Norway, Dorchester Town and Barnet before retiring due to injury.

Chivers then became mine host at the Brookmans Park Hotel in Hertfordshire, while more recently he has been heard providing expert opinions during live football commentaries on BBC Radio 5, in between organising the ex-Spurs Charity XI.

# RAY CLEMENCE

Goalkeeper
Born 5.8.48, Skegness

**LEAGUE RECORD**

| | A | G |
|---|---|---|
| Scunthorpe United | 48 | 0 |
| Liverpool | 470 | 0 |
| Tottenham Hotspur | 240 | 0 |

**HONOURS**
League Champions 1972/73,
   1975/76, 1976/77, 1978/79,
   1979/80
FA Cup 1973/74, 1981/82
League Cup 1980/81
European Cup 1976/77, 1977/78,
   1980/81
UEFA Cup 1972/73, 1975/76,
   1983/84
European Super Cup 1977
61 England caps

It was Bill Shankly who paid Scunthorpe United £18,000 for the nineteen-year-old RAY CLEMENCE, who had made forty-eight appearances for the Irons in the lower divisions. Shankly's later assessment of the man was that he was possibly the most important factor in Liverpool's continued success throughout the seventies. Indeed, Clemence only missed six matches during that period.

Clemence had to wait two and a half seasons before clinching a place in the Reds' first team, as Tommy Lawrence's consistent form kept him out. But, once in, he immediately impressed with safe handling and sharp reflexes. He got down quickly to low shots, knew when not to come off his line, and had great positional sense. In his first full season he conceded only twenty-two goals in forty-one games, helping the Reds equal the First Division record of twenty-four in a season. In 1978/79 he was even better, letting in only sixteen goals.

Of course, being behind one of the world's best defences, he needed to have great powers of concentration. He was kept idle for long periods, not getting a touch of the ball. It was a measure of his greatness that when he did have to respond, he would produce a top-class save. Of lightweight build and very athletic, he was able to spring several feet into the air and claim the ball with a very safe pair of hands. He was also one of the first goalkeepers to act as a sweeper behind his defence, leaving his penalty area to cut out the long through-ball.

His world-class saves were many but perhaps none was more important than one he pulled off in the 1975/76 UEFA Cup away leg at Dynamo Dresden. He saved a penalty by diving full-length to his right to reach a hard low shot and keep the tie goalless after ninety minutes. Liverpool went on to take the trophy.

He was unlucky to be around at the same time as Peter Shilton, for throughout his illustrious career at international level, in which he won sixty-one caps, he was always vying for the number 1 jersey with Shilts.

In August 1981, Clemence announced he was looking for a new challenge and moved to Spurs. He had hardly missed a match throughout his time at Anfield and had picked up more club honours than any other goalkeeper.

In his first season at White Hart Lane, he helped the club retain the FA Cup and reach the League Cup Final, where they lost to Liverpool. Injuries eventually began to affect his high level of performance and he was forced to retire.

After being appointed goalkeeping coach by Spurs, Ray had a spell as manager of Barnet before becoming England's full-time goalkeeping coach.

# RALPH COATES
Midfielder
Born 26.4.46, Hetton-le-Hole

Another of the seemingly endless stream of football talent that came to Burnley from the north-east in the 1960s, RALPH COATES was an extremely versatile player but at his best in a wide midfield role. Coates was surprisingly fast for such a stockily built man and his boundless energy and wholehearted approach to the game made him a popular figure at Turf Moor.

His reputation steadily grew, and in 1967 he was awarded the first of eight Under-23 caps. He later represented the Football League and in April 1970 he won his first England cap, when he replaced Francis Lee for the match against Northern Ireland. He was then named in the initial squad for the Mexico World Cup that summer, only to be omitted from the final twenty-two.

**FACT**

By beating Orient 7–3 away on 10 November 1979, Chelsea reached their 1000th win in Football League games. At the time it was their highest score in an away fixture.

Following Burnley's relegation in 1970/71, Coates joined Tottenham Hotspur. His time at White Hart Lane was both eventful and rewarding. He won two further caps for England, a UEFA Cup winners' medal in 1972, and a League Cup winners' medal in 1973, where Coates himself scored the only goal of the game against Norwich city.

Coates continued to be a first-team regular with Spurs for the next few seasons but left the club after their relegation to the Second Division in 1977.

After a short spell in Australia, he returned to League action with Orient. He enjoyed a new lease of life at Brisbane Road, making the number 11 shirt virtually his own property for over two seasons. In 1979/80 he was an ever-present and also had his best season in terms of goals scored, netting nine, including two against his former club, Burnley.

In 1982 he joined Orient's coaching staff and later played non-League football for Hartford Heath and Ware, whom he also managed.

A player who will always be fondly remembered by fans at all his clubs as a great team man, Ralph Coates went on to run a catering business and manage a leisure complex in Hertfordshire, but he is now manager of the Marconi Sports Club in Chelmsford. He also still occasionally turns out for charity soccer matches.

# STEVE COPPELL

Winger
Born 9.7.55, Liverpool

**LEAGUE RECORD**

| | A | G |
|---|---|---|
| Tranmere Rovers | 35 (3) | 10 |
| Manchester United | 320 (2) | 54 |

**HONOURS**
Second Division Champions 1974/75
FA Cup 1976/77
42 England caps

STEVE COPPELL's football career didn't conform to the normal pattern. He was studying Economics at Liverpool University when Tranmere Rovers rated him highly enough to play him as an amateur in their Third Division side. After just thirty-eight appearances for the Prenton Park side, his enormous potential was spotted by the then top team of Division Two, Manchester United, and in February 1975 Tommy Docherty signed him for £30,000.

It was the time when wingers were just coming back into fashion and Coppell became one of the new breed of wide midfield players.

Coppell established himself in United's team almost at once and progressed to international level almost immediately. He appeared once in the England Under-23 side before winning the first of forty-two full caps against Italy in 1977.

Steve Coppell could wriggle past defenders, race to the touchline and send over a perfect cross, but he could also chase back and provide cover for his defenders. He also had a knack of cutting in from the right flank and hitting some waist-high drives.

He gained an FA Cup winners' medal in 1977 and, though he was not a particularly noted goal-scorer, he ended the 1978/79 season as joint top-scorer with eleven goals. Noted for his all-action, never-say-die attitude, his career was brought to an early end by a tackle from the Hungarian defender Joseph Toth at Wembley in November 1981.

He struggled on for another fourteen months, producing some of his best ever football and undergoing three operations, but there was no way back. He was able to play in the first four games of the 1982 World Cup Finals but the problem flared up again in the goalless draw against West Germany. Following this serious knee injury, he was forced to retire on medical advice – he had enjoyed only ten years at the top but he had made quite an impression.

In June 1984 he turned to management with Crystal Palace, showing the same enthusiasm that he did while Chairman of the PFA, making him, at twenty-eight, the youngest League manager. Tipped to be a future England manager, he resigned in 1993 and became Chief Executive of the Football League Managers Association, a post he held until March 1995. He then returned to Selhurst Park as technical director, before being enticed in October 1996 into becoming manager of Manchester City. He then had two more periods (1997/98 and 1999/2000) in charge

of Crystal Palace before taking over the reins at Brentford in 2001. Now in charge at Brighton and Hove Albion, Steve Coppell is respected not only for his prowess as a winger, but for his integrity and intelligent views on the game.

# JOE CORRIGAN
Goalkeeper
Born 18.11.48, Manchester

**LEAGUE RECORD**

|  | A | G |
|---|---|---|
| Manchester City | 476 | 0 |
| Brighton & Hove Albion | 36 | 0 |
| Norwich City | 3 | 0 |
| Stoke City | 9 | 0 |

**HONOURS**
League Champions 1967/68
FA Cup 1968/69
League Cup 1969/70, 1975/76
European Cup Winners Cup 1969/70
9 England caps

All JOE CORRIGAN wanted to do from the age of four was to be a goalkeeper, so when he got the opportunity to go to Maine Road in 1966, he leapt at it even though he came from the Red area of Manchester! After being singled out in the club trials, where he gave some highly impressive performances, he turned professional in January 1967.

His first-team debut for Manchester City was in the Football League Cup tie against Blackpool at Maine Road in October of that year. The game ended all square at 1–1, but although he had kept his side in the game with a number of important saves, he had to wait until March 1969 for his Football League debut at Portman Road, where Ipswich beat City 2–1.

**FACT**

On 26 April 1971, Liverpool drew 2–2 away to Manchester City in Division One but were fined a then record £7,500 for fielding a weakened team.

In his early days, he was always in the shadow of Harry Dowd and Ken Mulhearn, and when he did get a chance he was inconsistent. Despite this unimpressive start to his league career, he fought hard to establish himself but faced another crisis of confidence when, in 1973, City signed Keith MacRae from Motherwell. Out of favour with the then City manager Ron Saunders, he asked for a transfer and was transfer-listed in February 1974. However, once again the 6ft 4in keeper buckled down and won back his first-team place, going on to serve City for a further nine years.

Manchester City have had three outstanding keepers since the war – Frank Swift, Bert Trautmann, and Joe Corrigan. His best season for City was 1976/77, when he conceded only thirty-four goals in his forty-two appearances, keeping twenty-two clean sheets.

He won League Cup honours in 1970 and 1976 and a European Cup Winners' Cup medal in 1970, when City beat Gornik Zabrze 2–1. When City played Spurs at Wembley in the 1981 FA Cup Final, Corrigan had looked unbeatable – the game ending at 1–1. For his heroics between the posts, Corrigan was named Man of the Match, but he was beaten three times in the replay as the White Hart Lane club won 3–2.

Corrigan played in 476 League games for Manchester City and in another 116 Cup matches, making him second only to Alan Oakes in terms of the number of first-team appearances for City. In March 1983 City transferred him to Seattle Sounders in the NASL for £30,000. He later returned to these shores to play for Brighton and Hove Albion, Norwich City and Stoke City.

He then coached goalkeepers at a number of clubs including Celtic, Middlesbrough, Tranmere Rovers and Barnsley, before being offered a post at Anfield as Liverpool's first full-time goalkeeping coach.

# TONY CURRIE
Midfielder
Born 1.1.50, Edgware

**HONOURS**
17 England caps

One of the country's most gifted midfielders, TONY CURRIE was artistic on the ball and blessed with great vision. He signed amateur forms with Queens Park Rangers while working for a building company, was rejected by Chelsea after a brief spell as an apprentice and was then picked up by Watford in May 1967, when he also won England youth honours. He emerged spectacularly from his Watford apprenticeship with six goals in his first four league games, but soon after his eighteenth birthday he joined Sheffield United for a fee of £35,000.

He scored on his Blades debut in a 3–2 defeat of Tottenham Hotspur but was unable to play in the next match because it was his wedding day! Currie was soon pushing for England recognition, although the Blades were not then a fashionable club. He played for the Football League XI and England Under-23s and won the first of seventeen full caps in 1972 when he played against Northern Ireland. Currie scored many spectacular goals during his stay at Bramall Lane, and in September 1973 netted two in a 5–0 defeat of Arsenal. During the course of this game, Currie, who was in devastating form, sat on the ball, completing United's revenge for a 5–0 home defeat by the Gunners two seasons previously. Later that season, in a bid to curb his brushes with authority, Currie was made Sheffield United captain – but it didn't change him: in the game with Leicester City, he and Alan Birchenall exchanged kisses!

Sheffield United eventually succumbed to a £245,000 bid by Leeds United and Currie maintained his star status at Elland Road by adding consistency to his talents. He was the nearest thing Leeds had to fill the vacuum created by the departure of the Bremner–Giles combination.

For two seasons he was a regular in the England squad but could not add domestic honours. His wife became unsettled and he returned to London to join Queens Park Rangers, helping them to the 1982 FA Cup Final before injuries checked his progress.

After brief periods with Toronto Nationals and Chesham United he joined Southend and then Torquay United as a non-contract player. In October 1981 he joined Tranmere but was released before making a senior appearance. After spells with non-League Dunstable, Hendon and Goole Town, Tony Currie was appointed full-time community organiser at Sheffield United.

# ALAN CURTIS

Forward/Midfielder
Born 16.4.54, Pentre

A nephew of former Swansea, Manchester City and Welsh international Roy Paul, ALAN CURTIS was taken on to the Swansea ground staff directly from school and soon emerged as a first-team player of skill, vision and imagination. Curtis became quite a prolific marksman, netting his first first-team hat-trick in a 4–1 Welsh Cup win over Newport County in January 1977. His first League hat-trick came in a 5–0 defeat of Crewe Alexandra in November 1977, and five months later both Curtis and Robbie James scored hat-tricks as the Swans recorded their biggest-ever League win, beating Hartlepool United 8–0.

Curtis built his reputation as Swansea surged out of the lower reaches of the League, and in May 1979 he joined Leeds United for £400,000, a record for a player from the lower divisions. Though injury restricted his career with the Yorkshire club to eighteen months, he did provide a handful of memorable moments. In October 1979, Leeds, who had endured six months without an away win, travelled to Southampton. Curtis scored a glorious individual goal in the dying seconds of the game, running almost the full length of the pitch to drive home a long-range shot that gave Leeds a 2–1 victory.

Curtis returned to the Vetch Field in December 1980 when Swansea paid £165,000 to take him back to South Wales. He went on to be an important member of the side that won promotion to the First Division for the first time in club history.

He left the Vetch for a second time in November 1983, following the club's relegation from the top flight – joining Southampton for £85,000 to ease the Swans' financial plight. Unable to find his best form on the south coast, he was loaned to Stoke City, but things didn't work out for him and he returned to South Wales, this time to play for Cardiff City. In 1987/88 he was instrumental in the club winning promotion to the Third Division and the Welsh Cup. Yet during the early part of the following season he returned to the Vetch Field for a third spell!

He announced his retirement at the end of the 1989/90 season, having scored 96 goals in 364 league games for the Swans. He then had spells with Barry Town and Haverfordwest before working as a financial consultant for a life insurance company and later returned to the Vetch Field as assistant to John Hollins.

## LEAGUE RECORD

| | A | G |
|---|---|---|
| Manchester United | 107 (4) | 23 |
| Derby County | 111 (1) | 31 |
| Coventry City | 82 (2) | 19 |
| Leicester City | 17 | 1 |
| Birmingham City | 31 (1) | 1 |
| Shrewsbury Town | 55 | 8 |
| Stoke City | 17 (5) | 1 |
| Doncaster Rovers | 37 (2) | 4 |

## HONOURS

Second Division Champions
  1974/75
47 Republic of Ireland caps

# GERRY DALY
## Midfielder
### Born 30.4.54, Dublin

Much travelled midfielder GERRY DALY was one of the stars of Tommy Docherty's Manchester United side after his arrival from Dublin club Bohemians for £12,500 in April 1973.

His time at Old Trafford was a mixture of joy and despair. He was a fringe member of the side relegated from the top flight in 1973/74, an integral member of the team which won the Second Division Championship the following season, and a losing Wembley finalist in 1976, when United were beaten 1–0 by Southampton in the FA Cup Final.

United's regular penalty-taker, he had scored thirty-two goals in 142 League and Cup games for the club when a disagreement with the manager brought his Old Trafford career to an end. In March 1977, Derby County manager Colin Murphy stepped in to secure his services for a fee of £190,000, making him Ireland's most expensive player at that time.

Daly made an immediate impact at the Baseball Ground. His hard work and battling qualities helped the club to a position of mid-table security. However, only months after Daly had put pen to paper, Tommy Docherty arrived to take over the reins at Derby and Daly immediately asked for a transfer. The request was later withdrawn, but the two men had an uneasy relationship. In August 1980, Daly, who had scored 31 goals in 112 League games was sold by new manager Colin Addison to First Division rivals Coventry City for £300,000.

> **FACT**
>
> On 27 November 1974, Derby County were playing Velez Mostar in the UEFA Cup third-round first-leg game at the Baseball Ground and losing 1–0. Manager Dave Mackay sent on both substitutes: Jeff Bourne and Alan Hinton. Bourne scored twice and Hinton once to give the Rams a 3–1 win.

Daly spent four years at Highfield Road, during which time he had a brief loan spell with Leicester City, helping the Foxes win promotion to the First Division in 1983/84.

In August 1984 he was transferred to Birmingham City for just £10,000 – the fee being set by a tribunal. Exactly a decade after helping Manchester United win the Second Division title, he helped the St Andrew's club win promotion to the top flight.

Daly later played for Shrewsbury Town and Stoke City before signing for his

final League club, Doncaster Rovers. Not content with donning the colours of eight Football League clubs, Gerry also spent May 1973 and May 1979 with New England Tea Men in the NASL.

Daly, who had few equals as a midfield player, also won forty-seven full caps for the Republic of Ireland. At the beginning of the 1990/91 season he became player-manager of Vauxhall Conference club Telford United, a post from which he was dismissed in October 1993. Sadly, he is now unable to work because of a back problem.

## LEAGUE RECORD

| | A | G |
|---|---|---|
| West Ham United | 194 | 0 |
| Leyton Orient | 170 | 0 |
| Aston Villa | 30 | 0 |
| Leeds United | 227 | 0 |
| Luton Town | 4 | 0 |
| Sheffield United | 1 | 0 |
| Carlisle United | 16 | 0 |

## HONOURS
FA Cup 1974/75
Second Division Champions 1989/90

# MERVYN DAY
Goalkeeper
Born 26.6.55, Chelmsford

Hailed as a future England goalkeeper after a breathtaking start to his career, MERVYN DAY made his West Ham United debut as a replacement for Bobby Ferguson in a match against Ipswich town on a rainy night at Upton Park in August 1973. After only two games in the first team, Hammers boss Ron Greenwood declared that Day would be the club's goalkeeper for the next ten years. Though that wasn't to be the case, Day did go on to appear in 231 League and Cup games before leaving Upton Park.

In 1975 he won an FA Cup winners' medal when as the youngest ever keeper in this Wembley showpiece, he kept a clean sheet in a 2–0 win over Fulham. The same year he was named PFA 'Young Player of the Year'. After being ever present in 1976/77, Day had to share the goalkeeping duties over the next two seasons with the recalled Ferguson. The relegation battle in 1977/78 also did little for Mervyn Day's confidence, any little mistake being blown out of all proportion by the media.

Following the signing of Phil Parkes in February 1979, Day moved to Orient for a fee of £100,000. He turned in some memorable performances for the 'O's and, in October of that year, he was selected as substitute goalkeeper for England 'B' in their match against New Zealand at Brisbane Road.

Aston Villa then signed him as cover for Nigel Spink before Eddie Gray took him to Leeds for just £30,000 in February 1985.

He was a key figure in United's run to the 1987 FA Cup semi-final and in 1989/90, when Leeds won the Second Division Championship, he made his 600th League appearance. Following John Lukic's arrival, Day spent his last season at Elland Road as the club's player-coach.

In July 1993 he joined Carlisle United as their player-coach after loan spells with both Luton Town and Sheffield United. The Cumbrian club won the Third Division Championship in 1994/95 and lost 1–0 to a sudden-death goal against Birmingham City in the Auto Windscreen Final at Wembley.

In February 1996, Day stepped up to become Carlisle's manager but lost his job the following year. He is now first-team coach at Charlton Athletic.

Mervyn Day, an outstanding goalkeeper in his day.

## LEAGUE RECORD

|  | A | G |
|---|---|---|
| Burnley | 406 (4) | 63 |
| Everton | 190 | 29 |
| Bury | 60 (1) | 4 |

## HONOURS
Second Division Champions
  1972/73
Third Division Champions 1981/82
5 England caps

# MARTIN DOBSON
## Midfielder
### Born 14.2.48, Blackburn

One of the most elegant and stylish players to wear the claret and blue of Burnley, MARTIN DOBSON was very nearly lost to the professional game when Bolton Wanderers gave him a free transfer in 1967.

He was on the verge of giving the game up when his father persuaded Burnley manager Harry Potts to give him a trial at Turf Moor. He impressed sufficiently to be offered a contract and within a month of putting pen to paper, he was playing in the Clarets First Division side.

Although he started his career as a centre-forward, it was only when he moved into midfield that he really found his true position.

By the start of the 1970s, Martin Dobson was now captaining the Burnley side and in 1972/73 the Clarets swept to the Second Division Championship. Sixth place in the top flight in 1973/74, and an FA Cup semi-final spot, helped Dobson win full international honours, with his first cap coming against Portugal in Lisbon, four days after the semi-final defeat.

Then, in August 1974, Everton smashed the British transfer record, paying the Clarets £300,000 for Dobson's services.

In five years on Merseyside, Dobson was a regular in the Everton side, which was only modestly successful by Goodison Park standards. He figured in two UEFA Cup campaigns and, in 1977, played in the FA Cup semi-final defeat by Liverpool and the three-game marathon in the League Cup Final, which ended in defeat by Aston Villa at Old Trafford.

Dobson was thirty-one when, in the summer of 1979, he returned to Turf Moor. Unable to prevent Burnley's relegation from the Second Division, he captained the club to the Third Division Championship. Following the arrival of John Bond as manager, Dobson was allowed to join Bury, later becoming the Shakers' player-manager.

In 1984/85 he led the Gigg Lane club to promotion from Division Four, but four years later he left to take over the reins at Bristol Rovers. On leaving the Pirates, he coached youngsters in the north-west prior to his appointment as manager of Unibond League club Chorley in 1995. A year later, he returned to Burnden Park, then the home of Bolton Wanderers, where he became the club's Youth Development Officer. Nowadays, Martin Dobson is a scout.

# WILLIE DONACHIE
Left-back
Born 5.10.51, Glasgow

Manchester City were the reigning League Champions when WILLIE DONACHIE joined the Maine Road club in 1968. It was as a long-term replacement at left-back for broken-leg victim Glyn Pardoe that Donachie, a former Celtic ground-staff boy, really established himself.

Donachie's skill and class were soon noticed by the international selectors. After appearing three times for Scotland's Under-23 side, he made his full international debut against Peru at Hampden Park in April 1972, eventually gaining thirty-five Scotland caps. He was a virtual ever-present during his eleven years at Maine Road, all of them in the top flight. He played in two League Cup Finals, collecting a winners' medal in 1976 as Newcastle United were defeated at Wembley. He also played in every game in 1976/77, when City were beaten to the League Championship by a single point by Liverpool.

**FACT**

The Manchester derby at Old Trafford on 27 April 1974 was abandoned five minutes before time when spectators invaded the pitch after City had scored the first goal. The result was allowed to stand. United lost 1–0 and were relegated after thirty-six years in the top flight. City's scorer was Denis Law – a former United player!

In March 1980, City accepted a fee of £200,000 from Portland Timbers and so Donachie took his skills across the Atlantic. After a brief return to help Norwich City win promotion to the First Division in 1982, he rejoined Portland before Burnley secured his services in November of that year. After a couple of seasons at Turf Moor, Donachie joined Oldham Athletic in the summer of 1984, later becoming the Latics' player-coach. He continued to play for the Boundary Park club until 1991, when the Latics clinched the old Second Division Championship. When he played his last league game, he was three months past his 39th birthday.

Willie Donachie's partnership with manager Joe Royle was a major factor in Oldham's success. When Royle was appointed Everton boss in 1994, Donachie became his assistant. The pair guided the Blues to success over Manchester United in the 1995 FA Cup Final before Royle lost his job in 1997.

Appointed manager of Manchester City, Royle again wanted Donachie, so he returned to Maine Road as City's head coach. After a spell as first-team coach at Sheffield Wednesday, Donachie has teamed up with Royle again, this time at First Division Ipswich Town.

# MICKY DROY
## Central Defender
### Born 7.5.51, Highbury

**LEAGUE RECORD**

|  | A | G |
|---|---|---|
| Chelsea | 263 (9) | 13 |
| Luton Town | 2 | 0 |
| Crystal Palace | 49 | 7 |
| Brentford | 19 | 3 |

**HONOURS**
European Cup Winners Cup 1970/71
Second Division Champions
   1983/84

MICKY DROY played his early football with non-League Slough Town before moving to Stamford Bridge in October 1970. The rough edges were very apparent in his first few seasons in south-west London and it was halfway through the 1973/74 season before he established himself in the Chelsea side. It was during the course of the following season, as the Blues slipped towards relegation to Division Two, that Droy's courageous and aggressive

displays at the heart of the Chelsea defence proved inspirational. When Micky Droy ran out on the pitch for away games in those early days, his sheer size – 6ft 4in and well over fifteen stone – presented an imposing sight and drew gasps of astonishment from the home fans.

In 1975/76 he was hampered by a series of niggling injuries that cost him his place in the side and he was replaced by Steve Wicks. Chelsea won promotion that season and in 1976/77, as they struggled hard to avoid relegation, manager Ken Shellito decided to use Droy and Wicks – both towering defenders – alongside each other in the heart of the Blues' defence. The partnership proved very effective and Micky Droy was named as the supporters' Player of the Year.

Over the next couple of seasons he became much more authoritative and, as his reading of the game improved, his lack of speed was rarely punished. Often sent upfield to remedy desperate situations, Droy didn't score too many goals but he certainly created chances for others.

Micky Droy succeeded Ray Wilkins as Chelsea captain and his influence on a young Chelsea side over the next four seasons or so was invaluable. He always played with total commitment and in doing so missed almost a quarter of Chelsea's matches with injuries. However, when he was fully fit, Micky Droy was utterly dominant, particularly when the ball was in the air.

Following the arrival of Joe McLaughlin, Micky Droy, who had appeared in 313 games for the Blues, left Stamford Bridge to continue his career with Crystal Palace. He did a fine job at Selhurst Park before ending his first-class career with Brentford.

He was then involved for a good number of years with Kingstonian FC, first as player-coach and then as manager, before becoming the director of an electrical wholesalers in Willesden.

## LEAGUE RECORD

| | A | G |
|---|---|---|
| Tottenham Hotspur | 101 (2) | 53 |
| Derby County | 35 (1) | 12 |
| Scunthorpe United | 3 (6) | 0 |

# JOHN DUNCAN
Forward
Born 22.2.49, Dundee

JOHN DUNCAN, who used to stand on the terraces at Dundee, turned professional for his home-town club on leaving school. As a junior he was farmed out to Broughty Athletic but it wasn't long before he was in the Dundee team. Showing an eye for goal, he was twice selected as a non-playing substitute for the full Scotland side before making a Scottish League appearance against the Football League in March 1973, when he scored both goals in a 2–2 draw.

In 1974 he won a Scottish League Cup winners' medal when Dundee beat Celtic 1–0 in the final, but in October of that year he became Terry Neill's first signing for Tottenham Hotspur – a fee of £150,000 taking him to White Hart Lane.

He was an immediate success, his twelve goals in his first season making him top scorer and effectively keeping Spurs in the First Division.

Though he wasn't the greatest of footballers when away from goal, John Duncan was absolutely lethal in the penalty area, where his speed of reaction with either foot and with his head made him both a deadly and regular goal-scorer. Duncan led the club's scoring chart again the following season but a serious back injury saw him miss most of the 1976/77 campaign, when his goals may well have saved the North London club from the ignominy of relegation to Division Two.

Duncan was back to his best in 1977/78, finishing the season as the club's leading scorer again and helping Spurs return to the top flight at the first attempt.

Duncan went on to score 75 goals in 145 League and Cup games for Spurs before, in September 1978, he joined Derby County for a fee of £150,000.

Recurring back-injury problems restricted Duncan to only thirty-seven appearances for the Rams and he moved to Scunthorpe United, quickly taking over as manager. Harshly sacked by the Irons to make way for Allan Clarke, he joined Hartlepool United; but after only two months in charge he moved to Chesterfield, and led them to the 1984/85 Fourth Division Championship. In June 1987 he joined Ipswich Town, where, despite the Suffolk team's reputation for bright, adventurous football, he became the first Ipswich manager to be dismissed, when they failed to make the 1990 promotion play-offs.

After a spell in radio journalism and teaching, he was once again appointed manager of Chesterfield, and in 1996/97 led them to the FA Cup semi-finals. Duncan, who was also involved with the League Management Association, remained at Saltergate until being replaced by Nicky Law.

John Duncan, a persistent and determined footballer.

## LEAGUE RECORD

|  | A | G |
|---|---|---|
| Liverpool | 64 (34) | 34 |
| Norwich City | 1 (1) | 0 |
| Oldham Athletic | 6 (11) | 1 |
| Tranmere Rovers | 3 (11) | 1 |
| Wigan Athletic | 4 (3) | 1 |

## HONOURS

League Champions 1975/76, 1976/77,
 1979/80
European Cup 1977/78
UEFA Cup 1975/76
European Super Cup 1977

# DAVID FAIRCLOUGH
## Forward
### Born 5.1.57, Liverpool

Better known as 'Super Sub', there is no doubt that DAVID FAIRCLOUGH was at his most effective in the number 12 shirt. Though he made his League debut in November 1975, he caused his first sensation the following spring, when his goals turned the title race in Liverpool's favour. Coming on as a substitute, he won the points in the games at Anfield against Burnley, Everton and Stoke City – his winner in the Merseyside derby coming in the final minute of the game.

Tall, gangly and carrot-haired, David Fairclough was unmistakable. He was quick and dangerous, prepared to run at defences and carry the ball into the penalty area. It was very difficult to shake him off the ball and he had the knack of being in the right scoring place.

In the following season's European Cup quarter-final against St Etienne at Anfield, the French side were holding the advantage of an away goal when Fairclough replaced John Toshack. Five minutes from time he received a pass from Ray Kennedy and dribbled past three defenders before slipping the ball under the advancing keeper to put the Reds into the semi-finals. After that, Bob Paisley began to name him in his starting line-up with more frequency.

However, despite his many attributes, Fairclough really had only one season as a Liverpool regular. That was 1977/78, when he ended the campaign with a European Cup winners' medal – a personal highlight in his career.

Sadly, Fairclough's overall form was patchy: in the games that he did start, he had a tendency to drift out of the action, seeming to lack both stamina and concentration. As new players began to arrive at Anfield, he began to slip out of contention; but even when he did return for the odd game, he continued to frustrate a section of the Liverpool crowd – one minute displaying a gloriously unexpected touch, the next fluffing the simplest of passes.

On leaving Liverpool he went to Canada to play for Toronto Blizzards, before playing for Swiss club Lucerne. On his return to England he turned out for Norwich City and Oldham Athletic before joining Belgian club Beveren SK.

In August 1985 he signed for Tranmere Rovers; but after a season in which he failed to establish himself as a first-team regular, he joined Wigan Athletic.

Here injuries restricted his appearances and he was forced to hang up his boots.

Though he will go down in history as a man of whom the public expected too much, Fairclough will always be remembered for the major role he played in Liverpool's assault on Europe.

David Fairclough is now a freelance journalist, having successfully completed a course run by the National Council for the Training of Journalists during his playing days.

## PAUL FLETCHER
### Forward
### Born 13.1.51, Bolton

**LEAGUE RECORD**

|  | A | G |
|---|---|---|
| Bolton Wanderers | 33 (3) | 5 |
| Burnley | 291 (2) | 71 |
| Blackpool | 19 (1) | 8 |

**HONOURS**
Second Division Champions 1972/73
Anglo-Scottish Cup 1978/79

PAUL FLETCHER was still a raw seventeen-year-old when he made his League debut for his home-town club Bolton Wanderers in November 1968, scoring in a 2–1 defeat at Crystal Palace. Though he scored in his next game against Charlton, Bolton didn't rush him, preferring to let his talents develop naturally. However, his potential had already been noted by a number of clubs and Burnley, desperate to halt their slide out of the top flight, offered a club record fee of £60,000. Bolton, who were at the wrong end of Division Two, were not in a position to resist and Fletcher was on his way to Turf Moor.

Bolton's general manager, the legendary Nat Lofthouse, was reluctant to lose such an outstanding prospect, saying, 'Burnley have got themselves a fine centre-forward who will be a star of the future.'

Perhaps too much was expected of him at first, however, because he couldn't prevent the Clarets from being relegated. But as the club adapted to life in Division Two, Fletcher began to repay the fee and the faith shown in him. He was Burnley's leading scorer for the next three seasons, netting fifteen during the club's Second Division Championship-winning season of 1972/73.

Impressing in the club's first season back in the First Division, he won international recognition, being capped four times by England at Under-23 level. That season also saw Fletcher score one of the most spectacular goals ever. It came in Burnley's 4–1 win at Leeds when, with his back to goal, he rose to meet Nulty's centre and, with an overhead bicycle kick, smashed the ball home. He continued his energetic hard-running displays, showing considerable ability in the air too, until a knee injury at West Ham in March 1975 kept him out of the game for eight months.

On his return he was still first choice and still scoring goals, helping Burnley win the Anglo-Scottish Cup in December 1978. But Billy Hamilton's arrival signalled the end of his Turf Moor career and he joined Third Division

> **FACT**
>
> Newcastle United's captain in the 1977/78 season, Geoff Nulty is credited with the latest goal ever known to have been scored in a Football League match. On 27 March 1971 he hit a dramatic equaliser for Burnley in a 2–2 Division One home draw against Ipswich Town. It was timed officially as having been scored one second from the finish.

Blackpool. Sadly, within months, he broke his leg and badly damaged the knee ligaments – it was the end of his playing career.

After a spell outside football, he became interested in the commercial and business side of the game and in 1991 was appointed chief executive of Huddersfield Town. He later took over a similar position with his first club Bolton Wanderers, masterminding the club's relocation from Burnden Park to the Reebok Stadium.

In recent years, he has built a deserved reputation as a very accomplished and amusing after-dinner speaker.

## LEAGUE RECORD

| | A | G |
|---|---|---|
| Burnley | 193 (9) | 19 |
| Leeds United | 152 (2) | 11 |
| Cardiff City | 32 | 0 |
| Doncaster Rovers | 45 (6) | 1 |
| Bury | 19 | 0 |
| Wrexham | 91 (9) | 5 |

## HONOURS

Second Division Champions
   1972/73
66 Wales caps

# BRIAN FLYNN
## Midfielder
### Born 12.10.55, Port Talbot

One of Turf Moor's favourite sons, BRIAN FLYNN was first spotted playing for Neath Boys by Cardiff City – but the Bluebirds let him slip through the net, enabling Burnley to sign him.

He made his league debut for the Clarets in a First Division match at Arsenal in February 1974, and by the following season had begun to establish himself in the Burnley midfield – his busy all-action style more than compensating for his lack of inches.

Flynn was only nineteen when he won the first of sixty-six full caps for Wales in a 5–0 win over Luxembourg in the European Championships at Swansea in November 1974. He was not a prolific scorer, scoring his first goal for his country (in his third international against Scotland in May 1975) before he first found the net in a League match (in Burnley's 3–2 win at Everton in January 1976).

After the Clarets' relegation to Division Two in 1976 it was always going to be difficult to hold on to Flynn and so it proved when the Welshman joined Leeds United for £175,000 in November 1977. He made an immediate impact, forging a superb midfield partnership with the great Tony Currie. Instant control, constructive use of the ball and sheer endeavour made Brian Flynn one of the best midfield players of that era, but it still has to be said that Leeds of the late 1970s were not the vintage Leeds under Don Revie.

Following a brief loan spell at Turf Moor, he rejoined Burnley in November 1982 and played his part in the club's epic cup campaigns of that season. He left for Cardiff in 1984, and after brief spells at Doncaster and Bury, then joined Limerick as player-coach.

After Flynn had worked on the Football in the Community scheme at Burnley, Wrexham manager Dixie McNeil took him to the Racecourse Ground in February 1988. When McNeil resigned during the early stages of the 1989/90 season, Flynn was asked to take over as player-manager. After two traumatic campaigns and a rock-bottom finish in 1990/91, Flynn and his Wrexham side made the football world sit up and take notice with a victory in the FA Cup over reigning League champions Arsenal. He led the Robins to promotion to the new

Second Division in 1992/93 and over the next nine seasons he demonstrated all the credentials needed in football management. Flynn, who was one of the longest-serving managers in the Football League when he parted company with Wrexham, is now in charge of Swansea City.

## GERRY FRANCIS
### Midfielder
### Born 6.12.51, Chiswick

Midfielder GERRY FRANCIS captained both club and country and would have won more than his twelve caps but for a series of niggling injuries.

He was a product of the Queens Park Rangers' youth scheme which was so successful in the late 1960s but despite regularly successful performances between 1969 and 1971 he did not gain promotion until 1972/73. The next three seasons, however, were among the most successful in QPR's history. In 1975/76 *Match of the Day* cameras witnessed a goal from Francis in Rangers' 2–0 defeat of Liverpool that eventually won the 'Goal of the Season' award.

Francis made his international debut for England in October 1974 against Czechoslovakia, and was made captain of the national side in 1975, with manager Don Revie saying that it was his for the next ten years! Francis remains the only Rangers player to have achieved that honour. In 1976, Francis suffered an injury that was to finish his international career and restrict his League football opportunities for the following two seasons. He fought back to become a regular again in 1978/79 but never quite regained his earlier form.

He then moved through a number of transfer deals, going to Crystal Palace in 1979 for £450,000 and returning to Shepherd's Bush in February 1980 for a £150,000 fee. He was next transferred to Coventry City in February 1982, assisting the Sky Blues in their fight against relegation.

Francis then moved into management with Exeter City, but after a nightmare start when the Devon club finished bottom of the Third Division, he was sacked, and spent the 1984/85 season as a non-contract player with Cardiff, Swansea and Portsmouth.

Moving on to Bristol Rovers, he took them to the old Second Division before being appointed chief coach at Queens Park Rangers in May 1991. In November 1994 he took over the reins at Tottenham Hotspur for three years before returning again to Queens Park Rangers for a further three-year period. In the summer of 2001, Francis returned for a second spell in charge of relegated Bristol Rovers.

In December 2001, Francis resigned his position as manager and Director of Football, and now the popular former player runs a successful antiques shop in Chertsey, Surrey.

# TREVOR FRANCIS

Forward
Born 19.4.54, Plymouth

## LEAGUE RECORD

| | A | G |
| --- | --- | --- |
| Birmingham City | 278 (2) | 119 |
| Nottingham Forest | 69 (1) | 28 |
| Manchester City | 26 | 12 |
| Queens Park Rangers | 30 (2) | 12 |
| Sheffield Wednesday | 2 (47) | 5 |

## HONOURS
League Cup 1978/79, 1990/91
European Cup 1978/79, 1979/80
European Super Cup 1980
52 England caps

In February 1979 TREVOR FRANCIS became Britain's first million-pound footballer when he signed for Nottingham Forest.

He began his career with Birmingham City, making his first-team debut at Cardiff City in September 1970 at the age of just sixteen years and 139 days. It is true to say he exploded onto the League scene, with fifteen goals in his first twenty-one games for the Blues – including four in the match against Bolton Wanderers in February 1971.

From the start, he displayed electrifying speed off the mark, intricate dribbling skills, a powerful shot and amazing self-confidence – qualities that were to remain his trademarks during a long and successful career.

Forming a prolific goal-scoring partnership with Bob Latchford, he helped Birmingham win promotion to the First Division in 1971/72. He continued to score goals on a regular basis with a best of twenty-five in 1977/78 – in fact, throughout the seventies, it seemed as though Trevor alone was keeping the Blues in the First Division. But with the team finally destined for the drop in 1978/79, he was whisked away to Nottingham Forest by Brian Clough after asking to leave St Andrew's.

Francis, who had by now scored 133 goals in 330 League and Cup games, was plagued by injuries at the City Ground. Even so, he scored the winning goal in the 1979 European Cup Final against Malmo. Just one week into the 1981/82 season, he joined Manchester City.

A year later he was on his way to Sampdoria, where he won an Italian Cup winners' medal. After a spell with Atlanta, he then signed for Glasgow Rangers. A Skol Cup winners' medal at Ibrox was followed by a return to League football with Queens Park Rangers. After a year as player-manager at Loftus Road, he joined Sheffield Wednesday as a player in January 1990. Unlucky to be relegated in 1989/90, Wednesday bounced back immediately the following season after finishing third, and also won the League Cup. After Ron Atkinson's departure, Francis took over the reins as player-manager in June 1991, and in his first season the Owls finished third in Division One. In 1992/93, Francis took the club to two domestic finals but there was nothing to show for all their efforts except losers' medals.

In May 1995 Francis was dismissed, and a year later he was appointed manager of Birmingham City. Although they came close to winning promotion to the Premiership, it didn't happen, and in November 2001 Francis lost his job. He is now in charge of First Division Crystal Palace.

# ARCHIE GEMMILL
Midfielder
Born 24.3.47, Paisley

**LEAGUE RECORD**

|  | A | G |
| --- | --- | --- |
| Preston North End | 93 (6) | 13 |
| Derby County | 324 | 25 |
| Nottingham Forest | 56 (2) | 4 |
| Birmingham City | 97 | 12 |
| Wigan Athletic | 11 | 0 |

**HONOURS**
League Champions 1971/72,
  1974/75
Texaco Cup 1971/72
European Cup 1978/79
43 Scotland caps

ARCHIE GEMMILL first arrived in England from St Mirren in June 1967, signing for Preston North End for a fee of £16,000. Though only 5ft 5in in height, Archie was one of the most combative midfield players of the 1970s.

After three years at Deepdale, Gemmill moved to Derby County for £60,000 and it was under Brian Clough's management that his career really began to take off. He played a highly significant part in proceedings when the Rams won the League Championship in 1971/72, even though Archie and his team-mates were lying on a Spanish beach at the time it was settled – having already completed their fixtures as rivals Arsenal and Liverpool fought in vain to snatch the title from their clutches. Gemmill won a second League Championship medal in 1974/75 and went on to appear in 261 league games for the Rams before moving across the East Midlands to Nottingham Forest in October 1977.

Manager of Nottingham Forest was Brian Clough, his former boss at the Baseball Ground. Gemmill was a non-stop ninety-minute competitor, at his best when running with the ball, and this industrious side to Gemmill's talents obviously appealed to Clough. He went straight into the Forest side and, in the thirty-four games he played, was only on the losing side twice. At the end of the campaign, Gemmill picked up his third League Championship medal. Then in 1978/79 he was instrumental in helping Forest reach the European Cup Final. However, he didn't play on the big day, being on the substitute's bench as Forest beat Malmo 1–0 in Munich.

A valued member of the Scotland squad, he played forty-three times for his country – and no one who saw his goal against Holland in the 1978 World Cup will ever forget it. He had already scored from the penalty spot to give the Scots a 2–1 lead when, in the 68th minute of this vital qualifying match, he picked up the ball wide on the right. He threaded his way through the Dutch defence, evading three strong challenges before shooting home past the diving Jongblood.

In August 1979 he was allowed to leave Forest to join Birmingham City. He later played for Wigan Athletic before returning to the Baseball Ground for a second spell.

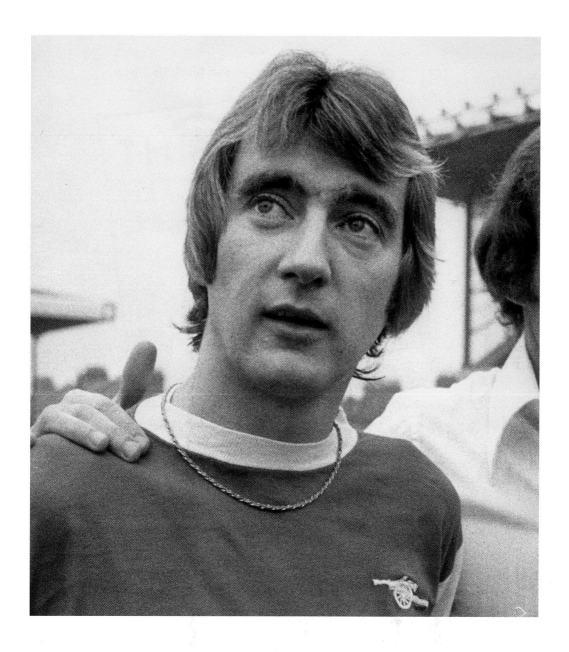

Highbury, picking up a losers' medal in the 1978 FA Cup Final before moving to the United States to play for Seattle Sounders.

In 1983 he rejoined Chelsea but illness and injury denied him the chance to show whether he could reproduce the magic of ten years before and he returned to the Victoria Ground for a second spell. After helping Stoke avoid relegation, a nagging knee injury forced his retirement.

The former owner of a nightclub, Alan Hudson now writes a controversial column in the *Sporting Life*, as well as working in other areas of the media and has not let himself be daunted by severe injuries suffered in a nearly fatal road accident a few years ago.

# EMLYN HUGHES

Defender/Midfielder
Born 28.8.47, Barrow

## LEAGUE RECORD

| | A | G |
|---|---|---|
| Blackpool | 27 | 1 |
| Liverpool | 474 | 35 |
| Wolves | 56 (2) | 2 |
| Rotherham Utd | 55 (1) | 6 |
| Hull City | 9 | 0 |
| Swansea City | 7 | 0 |

## HONOURS
League Champions 1972/73,
   1975/76, 1976/77, 1978/79
FA Cup 1973/74
European Cup 1976/77, 1977/78
UEFA Cup 1972/73, 1975/76
League Cup 1979/80
European Super Cup 1977
62 England caps

The son of a Welsh Rugby League star, EMLYN HUGHES decided that the round ball game was better suited to his talents. He began his career with Blackpool, making his debut against Blackburn Rovers in May 1966. Liverpool manager Bill Shankly was watching the game and made an offer straight after the match, but had to wait ten months before making his signing for £65,000.

Shanks predicted that one day Emlyn Hughes would lead England – and of course he was right. He was a natural for the job, his unbounding energy and infectious enthusiasm helping him to collect sixty-two caps.

He arrived at Anfield in February 1967 and in one of his early matches he brought down Newcastle forward Albert Bennett with a rugby tackle, causing him to be branded 'Crazy Horse' by the Kop – a nickname he will keep forever.

Though he played on the left side and was good with both feet, he was stronger on his right. His dynamic surges into the opposition's penalty box brought him a fair share of spectacular goals. One of these came against Southampton at Anfield in April 1971 when, after picking up the ball just outside his own area, he played it wide, stormed up the centre of the park to receive the return ball, then cracked home an unstoppable shot from the edge of the Saints' box.

A versatile player, in 1973/74 he moved to the centre of the Reds' defence and replaced Tommy Smith as captain. Although perhaps he wasn't as popular as Tommy, he was a great motivator and led by example. In his five seasons as captain, Hughes led Liverpool to two League Championships, two European Cups, the FA Cup and the UEFA Cup. Loved by the Anfield crowd, he was voted Footballer of the Year in 1978 and won more international caps as a Liverpool player than anyone else.

**FACT**

Emlyn Hughes holds the record for the highest number of first-class matches played in one season. In 1972/73 he made seventy-four appearances: forty-one for Liverpool in Division One, four in the FA Cup, eight in the League Cup, twelve in the UEFA Cup, eight internationals for England, and in the Common Market Entry match at Wembley for 'The Three' against 'The Six'.

In August 1979, having made 657 appearances in the famous red shirt, Hughes moved to Wolverhampton Wanderers. It came as no surprise when later that season they beat Nottingham Forest 1–0 at Wembley in the League Cup – it was the only club trophy Hughes needed to add to his collection. However, Emlyn began to suffer with knee trouble during his stay at Wolves and moved into the lower divisions, initially as player-manager with Rotherham United before playing for Hull City and Swansea.

An influential figure on the field during his successful years with Liverpool and England, Hughes's personality later earned him a nationwide reputation as a television celebrity on *Question of Sport*. Part-owner of a racehorse, he is now involved with a business incentive company selling items such as pens, T-shirts and bags.

# TOMMY HUTCHISON

Left Winger
Born 22.9.47, Cardenden

**LEAGUE RECORD**

|                   | A         | G  |
| ----------------- | --------- | -- |
| Blackpool         | 163 (2)   | 10 |
| Coventry City     | 312 (2)   | 24 |
| Manchester City   | 44 (2)    | 4  |
| Burnley           | 92        | 4  |
| Swansea City      | 163 (15)  | 9  |

**HONOURS**
Anglo-Italian Cup 1970/71
17 Scotland caps

TOMMY HUTCHISON was probably one of the most naturally gifted payers of the post-war era as well as being one of the most durable.

Blackpool manager Stan Mortensen brought him into League football in England from Alloa Athletic, recognising a rare talent that demanded a bigger stage. He immediately boosted the Seasiders' drive up the Second Division, only for promotion to the top flight to be denied on goal average. It was only a matter of time, however, and promotion was secured in 1970. But success was short-lived, and after just one season in the First Division, Blackpool were relegated.

Inevitably this attracted the big clubs and, in 1972, as Hutchison continued to impress with his close control and his ability to beat his man with skill and pace, Coventry City stepped in, offering cash and Billy Rafferty.

In 1973 he won the first of seventeen full Scottish caps, all won while with the Sky Blues. But the eight seasons he spent at Highfield Road were sadly barren in terms of domestic honours. In October 1980 John Bond signed him for Manchester City for £47,000.

From bottom of the First Division, the Blues progressed to a respectable mid-table finish in the League, the semi-final of the League Cup, and an epic FA Cup Final against Tottenham Hotspur. That final proved to be a bittersweet affair for the popular Scotsman, who headed City into a first-half lead only to have the misfortune to score a late equaliser for Spurs, deflecting a Glenn Hoddle shot past Joe Corrigan.

Tommy Hutchison left Maine Road in the summer of 1982 to spend a season in Hong Kong. He reappeared on the English scene the following year, new Burnley manager John Bond seeing him as one of the players he needed to respond to the challenge at Turf Moor. Never really accepted by the Burnley fans, he left to join Swansea in 1985, later becoming player-coach. He helped the Swans gain promotion to the Third Division in 1987/88 and then had a loan spell with Blackpool nearly twenty years after he had first played for the Seasiders.

At forty-two, he became the oldest player ever to play in a European tie, when Swansea competed in the European Cup Winners' Cup. At the end of his last

season in League football, he received a PFA Merit Award for his services to the game.

He is now the Football in the Community officer at Merthyr Tydfil, passing on some of his vast knowledge of the game at coaching sessions throughout the South Wales valleys.

# LEIGHTON JAMES
Left Winger
Born 16.2.53, Loughor, Glamorgan

**LEAGUE RECORD**

| | A | G |
|---|---|---|
| Burnley | 331 (5) | 66 |
| Derby County | 67 (1) | 15 |
| Queens Park Rangers | 27 (1) | 4 |
| Swansea City | 88 (10) | 27 |
| Sunderland | 50 (2) | 4 |
| Bury | 46 | 5 |
| Newport County | 21 (7) | 2 |

**HONOURS**
Second Division Champions 1972/73
Anglo-Scottish Cup 1978/79
54 Wales caps

One of the game's most naturally gifted players, LEIGHTON JAMES could easily have emerged as a Welsh Rugby international, excelling as he did at both the Association and Union codes during his schooldays.

The son of a Swansea steelworker, he began his career with Burnley, making his debut as a seventeen-year-old during the 1970/71 season. He was not a regular during that dismal campaign but his outstanding wing-play helped the Clarets youngsters reach the semi-final of the FA Youth Cup.

During the club's first season down in Division Two, his sparkling performances inevitably alerted the international selectors. He won his first Welsh cap in October 1971 against Czechoslovakia in Prague, the youngest ever Burnley international and one of the youngest players ever to be capped for Wales.

It was during the Clarets' 1972/73 Second Division Championship-winning season that Leighton James became a household name, his dazzling exhibitions of the winger's art stealing numerous shows. But after two good seasons back in the top flight, which included an FA Cup semi-final against Newcastle United at Hillsborough, the club began to struggle, and in November 1975 Leighton James joined Derby County for £310,000.

He became a regular at the Baseball Ground, but on the appointment of Tommy Docherty as manager he was sold to Queens Park Rangers for £180,000. But in less than a year he was back at Burnley, Harry Potts paying a club record £165,000 for his services.

Teaming up with Steve Kindon, who had also returned to the fold, he helped the Clarets win the Anglo-Scottish Cup – but after their relegation to Division Three in 1980 he moved again, this time to ambitious Swansea City.

He was an instant hit back in his homeland and was top scorer in their Second Division promotion-winning season. He also played a key role in the Swans' victory in the Welsh Cup, their passport to Europe.

James moved to Sunderland on a free transfer in January 1983, helping to spark something of a mini-revival as the Wearsiders' slide towards relegation was arrested.

He then returned to the north-west with Bury, helping the Shakers win promotion to Division Three, before passing a brief spell as Newport County's player-coach. In July 1986 he returned to Burnley for a third spell, playing his part in the Clarets' most dramatic season ever.

On hanging up his boots, he briefly coached Bradford City before spells as manager with non-League Gainsborough Trinity and Morecambe. A regular on radio sports programmes, where his knowledgeable and well-informed views on the football scene are compulsive listening, Leighton James is currently manager of South Wales club, Llanelli.

# DAVID JOHNSON

Forward
Born 23.10.51, Liverpool

**LEAGUE RECORD**

|  | A | G |
|---|---|---|
| Everton | 79 (11) | 15 |
| Ipswich Town | 134 (3) | 35 |
| Liverpool | 128 (20) | 55 |
| Barnsley | 4 | 1 |
| Manchester City | 4 (2) | 1 |
| Preston North End | 20 (4) | 3 |

**HONOURS**
League Champions 1976/77,
    1978/79, 1979/80,
    1981/82
European Cup 1976/77, 1977/78,
    1980/81
Texaco Cup 1972/73
European Super Cup 1977
8 England caps

One of the few players to have made the short journey both ways across Stanley Park, DAVID JOHNSON began his Football League career with Everton. But despite his early success, which included a hat-trick in an 8–0 win over Southampton, he was transferred in October 1971 to Ipswich Town, where he matured into a useful centre-forward, winning three England caps.

Then, in August 1974, Johnson joined Liverpool for a club record £200,000 and was pitched straight into first-team action. Quick, skilful and unselfish, and with a courageous approach, Johnson instantly endeared himself to the Kop. But Paisley was blessed with a large and gifted squad and in the course of his permutations over the next two seasons, Johnson was often the man to be left out. Though he also wasn't helped by a series of niggling injuries, he managed to collect a League Championship medal and figured in the Wembley defeat by Manchester United – but he missed out on European glory.

It wasn't until the spring of 1978 that Johnson began to look like his old self, but with the club's European Cup campaign reaching a climax, he strained knee ligaments and was sidelined for the rest of the season.

Just when it seemed Liverpool were going to discard him, Johnson's luck then changed and, after two lengthy spells in the side, he struck up an effective partnership with Kenny Dalglish that led to more England honours and a few new trophies for the Reds – Johnson won a European Cup winners' medal in 1981 plus a total of four League Championship medals. In two campaigns with the Reds, his sharp control, work rate and ability to take up good positions brought him thirty-seven goals in sixty-three starts, finishing the 1979/80 season with two goals at Aston Villa to secure a second successive Championship. After that his scoring rate diminished and following the emergence of Ian Rush, his first-team outings were limited.

In August 1982, Johnson's colourful career came full circle when he rejoined Everton for £100,000. However, the goal touch which at one time had made him one of the most feared strikers in Europe was missing. After a loan spell with Barnsley, he joined Manchester City. He then had a brief spell with Tulsa Roughnecks in the NASL before ending his first-class career with Preston North End.

David Johnson remains the only man to have scored a derby winner for both Everton and Liverpool and so occupies a unique place in Merseyside folklore.

Johnson still lives on Merseyside, where he works for an insurance company and is a trustee of the North-West Sports Aid Foundation.

# JOE JORDAN

Forward
Born 15.12.51, Carluke

**LEAGUE RECORD**

|  | A | G |
| --- | --- | --- |
| Leeds United | 139 (31) | 35 |
| Manchester United | 109 | 37 |
| Southampton | 48 | 12 |
| Bristol City | 38 (19) | 8 |

**HONOURS**
League Champions 1973/74
FA Cup 1971/72
Inter Cities Fairs Cup 1970/71
52 Scotland caps

Volatile Scotsman JOE JORDAN's toothless grin became a regular feature of the League circuit – usually after the muscular centre-forward had forced the ball into the back of the net!

Jordan originally worked in an architect's office and was rejected after a trial with West Bromwich Albion. He played for junior side Blantyre Victoria before being picked up by Morton in October 1968. After just a handful of games for the Greenock club, Jordan was recommended to Leeds United by Bobby Collins, and in October 1970 the Yorkshire club signed the eighteen-year-old for a bargain £15,000.

Although he endured long spells as a substitute, Leeds transformed him into an unselfish and inspirational leader, winning a League Championship medal in 1973/74. Jordan, who won fifty-two full caps for Scotland and scored the goal which took them to the 1974 World Cup Finals, also played for Leeds in the two losing European Cup Final teams of 1973 and 1975.

In January 1978, Jordan joined Manchester United for a then record fee of £350,000. A great favourite with the Old Trafford crowd, he had three good seasons with the Reds before he joined the exodus of British players to Italy, signing for AC Milan in the summer of 1981 for £175,000. He also played for Verona before Southampton brought him back to England in the 1984 close season for around £100,000.

Although he was the Saints' leading scorer in his first season on the south coast, he suffered a series of niggling injuries and, in February 1987, was allowed to join Bristol City as player-coach, eventually becoming their manager.

He steered the Robins to the 1988/89 Littlewoods Cup semi-final and the following season led the Ashton Gate club to promotion from the Third Division.

Jordan, the only Scot to have scored in three World Cup Finals, acted as the country's public relations officer in the 1990 World Cup in Italy. In September that year he was appointed manager of Hearts, who in 1991/92 were runners-up to Rangers. Unable to capitalise on that platform, he had a spell as assistant manager at Celtic before going to Stoke City as manager in November 1993. He endured a torrid time there and twelve months later returned to Ashton Gate for a second spell as Bristol City manager. He then became assistant to Northern Ireland manager Lawrie McMenemy, but is now involved with the media as a radio and television summariser.

# KEVIN KEEGAN
Forward
Born 14.2.51, Armthorpe

When Bill Shankly plucked KEVIN KEEGAN from the obscurity of the lower divisions in 1971, there were few who doubted the wisdom of the Liverpool manager's move. Signed for just £35,000 from Scunthorpe United, Keegan hit Anfield like a tornado. Converted from deep-lying winger to striker, he made his debut for the Reds against Notts County in the opening match of the 1971/72 season – and scored after just seven minutes.

His all-action approach won over the fans and he soon became the idol of the Kop. He was brave, quick and completely inexhaustible. And his understanding up front with John Toshack bordered on the telepathic!

Keegan's performance in the 1974 FA Cup Final against Newcastle United, when he scored two goals, was one of his best for the club, although there were the odd turbulent times too. On one occasion he was sent off with Leeds midfielder Billy Bremner at Wembley, and on another he was roughed up by the Belgrade police after walking out on England, having been dropped by Don Revie.

The European Cup Final of 1977 against Borussia Moenchengladbach was Keegan's last game in the red of Liverpool. His duel with Bertie Vogts, captain of Borussia and West Germany, was a classic – Vogts was reckoned to be the best man-to-man marker in the world but Keegan ran him ragged.

**FACT**

In August 1974 Kevin Keegan was sent off twice in five days, first for Liverpool in a friendly against Kaiserslautern in West Germany and then against Leeds United in the Charity Shield at Wembley.

In 1977 he answered the call of continental football and joined SV Hamburg in Germany for £500,000. It made him England's most expensive and best-paid player. During six years at Anfield Keegan had won three League Championship medals, two UEFA Cup winners' medals and European and FA Cup winners' medals.

His three years at Hamburg enhanced his game further, in particular teaching him to overcome man-to-man marking. Having already captained England, he went on to twice become European Footballer of the Year.

In February 1980, Southampton manager Lawrie McMenemy swooped to sign him, and during the 1980/81 season his twenty-six goals were sufficient to make

Keegan the leading scorer in the First Division, for which he was awarded the Shoot-Adidas 'Golden Boot'.

Keegan made sixty-three appearances for his country but didn't play again for England after the 1982 World Cup. This was a shame, because he still had a lot of football in him, as evidenced by a two-year spell at Newcastle United during which he led the Magpies back to Division One before deciding to retire.

Having become a folk hero on Tyneside, he was welcomed back with open arms when he was appointed Newcastle manager in February 1992. In 1992/93 they won the First Division Championship and, once in the Premiership, were never out of the top six, finishing runners-up on two occasions. Following his sudden resignation, Keegan then took charge of Fulham, later becoming England's caretaker manager. After taking the Cottagers to the Second Division Championship, he took on the poisoned chalice of the England job full-time but resigned after a home defeat by Germany and a disappointing European Championship. He is now back in club management with Manchester City.

# STEVE KEMBER
Midfielder
Born 8.12.48, Croydon

**LEAGUE RECORD**

| | A | G |
|---|---|---|
| Crystal Palace | 255 (5) | 36 |
| Chelsea | 125 (3) | 13 |
| Leicester City | 115 (2) | 6 |

**HONOURS**
Second Division Champions 1978/79

Tigerish midfielder STEVE KEMBER began his career with Crystal Palace, where he matured under Dick Graham, Arthur Rowe and Bert Head and quickly became an important part of Palace's sides in the late 1960s and early 1970s. He was an ever-present in the promotion-winning side of 1968/69 that gained a place in Division One. Then, when playing in the top flight, he shone as brightly as any of the players who opposed him, and he gained his first England Under-23 cap in October 1970 in recognition of his undisputed talent.

He had succeeded John Sewell as Crystal Palace captain when, in September 1971, he moved to Chelsea for a fee of £170,000, as Bert Head sought funds to reshape his squad for First Division survival.

At Stamford Bridge manager Dave Sexton asked him to play wide on the right rather than in his preferred position at the heart of the action. Unable to make much impression, he soon became a frustrated and bewildered figure. Once Sexton had departed, he was restored to the centre of midfield where his confidence quickly returned; but following Chelsea's relegation he left to continue his career in the top flight with Leicester City.

By the time he arrived at Filbert Street, Steve Kember had totted up almost 350 League appearances. However, he didn't last long under Jock Wallace's regime, and in October 1978 Terry Venables paid £50,000 to take him back to Selhurst Park.

Here Kember added his experience to the precocious skills of a young team seeking to put Palace back into Division One, his influence being an important feature in Palace winning the 1978/79 Second Division Championship.

In March 1980 he crossed the Atlantic to sign for Vancouver Whitecaps for a couple of seasons, but in the summer of 1981 he returned to Crystal Palace as the club's youth coach. He was then appointed manager in November 1981, charged with keeping the side in Division Two, following relegation the previous season. Although he succeeded, he was surprisingly replaced in the summer of 1982 by Alan Mullery.

He went on in the late 1980s to run a wine bar in Croydon before managing Vauxhall-Opel League side Whyteleafe. He then returned to Selhurst Park as a reserve team coach.

## LEAGUE RECORD

|  | A | G |
| --- | --- | --- |
| Arsenal | 156 (2) | 53 |
| Liverpool | 272 (3) | 51 |
| Swansea City | 42 | 2 |
| Hartlepool United | 18 (5) | 3 |

## HONOURS

League Champions 1970/71, 1975/76,
    1976/77, 1978/79, 1979/80
FA Cup 1970/71
Inter Cities Fairs Cup 1969/70
League Cup 1980/81
European Cup 1976/77, 1977/78,
    1980/81
UEFA Cup 1975/76
European Super Cup 1977
17 England caps

# RAY KENNEDY
## Midfielder/Forward
### Born 28.7.51, Seaton Delaval

RAY KENNEDY joined Arsenal as an apprentice in April 1968 after having been rejected by Port Vale and going to work in a sweet factory. Little did he realise at that time that he would become the most honoured player (in terms of medals won) in the history of English football.

He shot to fame after scoring one of Arsenal's goals in the 1969/70 season's two-legged Inter Cities Fairs Cup Final as the Gunners beat Anderlecht 4–3 on aggregate. He became a regular in the Arsenal side the following season, ending the campaign in which the club did the 'double' with twenty-six goals – as well as being selected for England's Under-23 side and winning the Rothman's Young Player of the Year award. He spent a further three seasons at Highbury, winning another FA Cup winners' medal in 1971/72 and six Under-23 caps.

> Probably the most important goal in an English derby game came at White Hart Lane in 1971 when Ray Kennedy scored in the 89th minute to silence the home crowd and give Arsenal the League Championship. The Gunners went on to do the 'double'.
>
> **FACT**

Ray Kennedy arrived at Anfield as Bill Shankly's last signing although injury kept him out of the first four games of the 1974/75 season. Impressing new manager Bob Paisley, he ousted Welsh international John Toshack from the starting line-up, scoring ten goals in twenty-four games. However, towards the end of the campaign, Paisley began to experiment, playing Kennedy behind the twin strike force of Keegan and the recalled Toshack. By November 1975, Kennedy was installed on the left side of Liverpool's midfield and over the next six years or so helped the Reds win ten major honours.

Though he was short of pace, Kennedy could change the emphasis of a game with a sweeping crossfield pass, though his deadliest attribute was the ability to make a late run into the box to finish off a move at the far post.

He scored some vital goals for Liverpool including a late strike against Bayern Munich in the 1981 European Cup semi-final and a second-half volley against Bruges when the Belgian side were 2–0 up in the 1976 UEFA Cup Final.

After being squeezed out of the Liverpool side by Ronnie Whelan, he joined Swansea City for a fee of £160,000. The Swans were unbeaten in Kennedy's first nine games but midway through the following season he returned to his native north-east to see out his career with Hartlepool United.

After a spell as a publican and a coaching appointment at Sunderland, it was revealed that Ray Kennedy was suffering from Parkinson's disease. Since then, he has spent his time raising public awareness of the illness.

## LEAGUE RECORD

|  | A | G |
| --- | --- | --- |
| West Ham United | 546 (5) | 18 |
| Southend United | 34 | 1 |

**HONOURS**
FA Cup 1974/75, 1979/80
Second Division Champions 1980/81
2 England caps

# FRANK LAMPARD
## Full-back
### Born 20.9.48, East Ham

One of the greatest players in West Ham United's postwar history, FRANK LAMPARD made his league debut for the Hammers against Manchester City at Upton Park in November 1967. Towards the end of that season, he broke his leg in a 2–1 win at Sheffield United but eventually recovered from this major setback to re-establish himself in the West Ham side.

International recognition soon followed with four England Under-23 caps, before he won the first of his two full caps against Yugoslavia in October 1972. He had to wait another eight years for his second cap, when former Hammers boss Ron Greenwood selected him to play against Australia in Sydney in May 1980.

Lampard won an FA Cup winners' medal in 1975 as West Ham beat Fulham 2–0, and he played in the European Cup Winners' Cup Final the following season. In that match against Anderlecht, the Hammers were 1–0 up with just minutes remaining before half-time when Lampard suffered the second major setback of his career. Attempting to play the ball back to Mervyn Day, he caught his studs in the turf and suffered a serious stomach injury. To make matters worse, the Belgian side equalised from the incident and went on to win 4–2. Lampard was immediately flown home for an emergency operation.

On a happier note, it was left-back Frank Lampard who scored the semi-final winner against Everton at Elland Road to take the Hammers through to the 1980 FA Cup Final against Arsenal. By now he was at the peak of his career, and in 1980/81 he won League Cup runners-up and Second Division Championship medals.

Having played in 660 League and Cup games for the Hammers during his eighteen seasons at Upton Park, the popular left-back was given a free transfer at the end of the 1984/85 season. Lampard then joined Southend United, who were then managed by former West Ham United and England captain Bobby Moore. He had made just thirty-eight appearances for the Roots Hall club when, following a spate of niggling injuries, he decided to hang up his boots.

He returned to Upton Park as assistant manager to Harry Redknapp but lost his job in the summer of 2001 when Redknapp joined Portsmouth as Managing Director.

Frank Lampard senior, whose son Frank Lampard junior currently plays for Chelsea and England.

## BOB LATCHFORD
### Forward
### Born 18.1.51, Birmingham

**LEAGUE RECORD**

|  | A | G |
|---|---|---|
| Birmingham City | 158 (2) | 68 |
| Everton | 235 (1) | 106 |
| Swansea City | 87 | 35 |
| Coventry City | 11 (1) | 2 |
| Lincoln City | 14 (1) | 2 |
| Newport County | 20 | 5 |

**HONOURS**
12 England caps

BOB LATCHFORD began his Football League career with Birmingham City, scoring twice on his debut in a 3–2 win over Preston North End in March 1969. After five years at St Andrew's, in which Latchford scored 84 goals in 194 games, Everton manager Billy Bingham paid a record fee of £350,000 for the Birmingham centre-forward, with Howard Kendall and Archie Styles going in the opposite direction.

A strong, burly centre-forward, he was a difficult man to shake off the ball and was also good in the air. He had the special knack of turning half-chances into goals and was Everton's leading scorer for four consecutive seasons from 1975.

At the outset of the 1977/78 campaign, the *Daily Express* announced that it would award £10,000 to the first player in the top two divisions of the Football League to reach thirty goals. In October of that season, Latchford scored four when Everton beat Queens Park Rangers 5–1 at Loftus Road. He also netted a hat-trick in a 6–0 home victory over Coventry City with winger Dave Thomas providing the crosses. Then, on 29 April 1978, in a 6–0 thrashing of Chelsea, Latchford scored the two goals he needed to become the first top-flight player for six years to score thirty. (It was a close call, for there were only eight minutes of the season left!) However, Latchford didn't receive anywhere near £10,000 – just £192 to be exact. It was part of the deal that £5,000 went to the Football League and PFA Benevolent Fund and Bob generously shared the remainder between all who had helped him to achieve his thirty-goal haul.

During that season Latchford also made his full England debut in a World Cup qualifying match against Italy at Wembley.

In the course of the 1978/79 season, he scored a stunning five goals as Everton trounced Wimbledon in a League Cup match. He remained at Goodison for a further three seasons after that memorable thirty-goal campaign, taking his tally of goals to 138 in 289 League and Cup games – the club's leading goal-scorer since the war.

When Howard Kendall returned to Everton as player-manager, Latchford was the first player to depart, joining Swansea City. He enjoyed mixed fortunes in South Wales but he did score thirty-two goals in 1982/83 before being given a free transfer and joining Dutch club Breda. Within five months he had returned to these shores and signed for Coventry City, leaving twelve months later to play for Lincoln City – before ending his League career with Newport County.

He then owned a clothes shop in Swansea before moving back to the Midlands. Living in Redditch, he worked for a firm selling nuts and bolts and was later a marketing manager for Ladbrokes. Following a spell as Birmingham City's Youth Development Officer, Bob Latchford is now living in Germany.

# ALEC LINDSAY
### Left-Back
### Born 27.2.48, Bury

**LEAGUE RECORD**

|  | A | G |
| --- | --- | --- |
| Bury | 126 | 14 |
| Liverpool | 168 (2) | 12 |
| Stoke City | 20 | 3 |

**HONOURS**

League Champions 1972/73, 1975/76, 1976/77
FA Cup 1973/74
European Cup 1976/77
UEFA Cup 1972/73, 1975/76
European Super Cup 1977
4 England caps

ALEC LINDSAY began his career with his home-town club, Bury. A former England youth international, he helped the Shakers win promotion to the Second Division in 1967/68 before joining Liverpool for a fee of £67,000 in March 1969.

Although the Anfield club had watched him on a number of occasions, they were never sure as to his best position. Indeed at Bury he was used as a wing-half, inside-forward, and even on the wing in a couple of games. After taking longer than most to settle with the Reds, he made his debut and several further unremarkable appearances in midfield before being switched to the left-back berth he was to grace so stylishly.

During Lindsay's early days at Anfield, Bill Shankly advised him that he was less than satisfied with his performances to date, reminding him that when he had been at Bury, he had left defenders in his wake with his speed and skill – to which the Reds defender replied, 'But, boss, that was not me.' A bemused Shankly turned to Bob Paisley and said, 'By Christ, Bob, we've signed the wrong man!'

In winning an FA Cup winners' medal against Newcastle United in 1974, Lindsay was in tremendous form. Prominent on the overlap, he drove a ferocious cross-shot past keeper Iam McFaul only to have his joy cut short by an offside whistle. He was probably at the peak of his form in 1974, when he was capped four times by England when Joe Mercer was caretaker-manager, his first game being a 2–2 draw with Argentina.

Unfortunately, Lindsay's form deteriorated shortly afterwards, mainly because of personal problems, and he was never the same player again. He signed for Stoke City in August 1977 but played only twenty games before trying his luck in the United States and Canada. His last club was Toronto Blizzards in 1979 before he turned his back on football for good.

For such a talented footballer, it is a tragedy that Lindsay's career ended at the age of thirty-one, although to be fair it was really over when he left Anfield two years earlier.

The former pig farmer then ran a public house, the Foundry Arms in Leigh.

# BRIAN LITTLE

Forward
Born 25.11.53, Horden

**LEAGUE RECORD**

| | A | G |
|---|---|---|
| Aston Villa | 242 (5) | 60 |

**HONOURS**
Third Division Champions
  1971/72
League Cup 1974/75, 1976/77
1 England cap

BRIAN LITTLE had one of the briefest debuts ever at international level when he replaced Mick Channon against Wales at Wembley in 1975 with just ten minutes to play. Even so, he helped set up England's second goal for David Johnson in a 2–2 draw.

On his debut for the Aston Villa first team in April 1972, he scored one of the goals in their 5–1 defeat of Torquay United. Still only seventeen, he also played an important part in the club's FA Youth Cup success when they beat Liverpool over two legs in the final.

Little went on to win League Cup winners' tankards in 1975 and 1977, scoring two of Villa's goals in the 3–2 win over Everton in the third match of that final at Old Trafford – with his match-winner coming in the dying seconds of injury-time. In 1974/75, Little was the Second Division's leading goal-scorer with twenty goals, including a hat-trick in a 5–0 win over Oldham Athletic.

During the 1979/80 season, a proposed £610,000 move to neighbours and rivals Birmingham City fell through on medical grounds; and sadly, at the end of the following season, Brian Little was forced to give up the game. He had scored eighty-two goals in 301 first-team appearances.

He had a spell working in Villa's promotions department but then moved to Molineux as Wolves' first-team coach, later replacing Sammy Chapman to become the club's caretaker manager. On losing out to Graham Turner, he joined Villa team-mate Bruce Rioch at Middlesbrough before leaving to manage Darlington.

He led the Quakers to the GM Vauxhall Conference title and back into the Football League, where they won the Fourth Division Championship. He then took charge at Leicester City and after three successive seasons of reaching the Wembley play-off finals, the Foxes eventually won promotion to the Premiership.

In November 1994, Little returned to his beloved Aston Villa as manager, and after a season of struggle secured their Premiership status on the final day of the campaign. He set about rebuilding the Villa side and was rewarded with victory in the League Cup Final at Wembley. He then had spells managing Stoke City and West Bromwich Albion, before taking charge of Hull City, from whom he parted company in 2002.

**LEAGUE RECORD**

| | A | G |
|---|---|---|
| Everton | 364 (26) | 48 |
| Sheffield Wed | 129 | 12 |
| Grimsby Town | 50 | 4 |

# MICK LYONS
## Central Defender
### Born 8.12.51, Liverpool

A player who once admitted that he would readily run through a brick wall to further the Everton cause, MICK LYONS spent many of his boyhood Saturdays on the Goodison terraces. Converted from teenage striker to central defender, Lyons made his senior debut away at Nottingham Forest in 1971. There then followed two in-and-out seasons before he established himself as a regular at the heart of the Blues' defence. Though for the most part he was content with halting opposition forwards, Lyons could be a potent attacking force too. Everton managers Billy Bingham and Gordon Lee both selected him for emergency spells at centre-forward. In 1973/74 he was the club's top scorer with eleven goals – testimony to his versatility.

It was around this time that he won international recognition, being selected for England at Under-23 and 'B' level. He was also made captain of his beloved Everton.

Throughout his Everton career, Lyons was never on the winning side in a derby match, missing the only two victories achieved by the Blues in this period. Against Liverpool in December 1973, he found the net with a majestic header only to have the goal disallowed. Even more excruciatingly, he volleyed a 40-yard own goal past a dumbfounded George Wood in a 2–2 draw at Anfield almost two years later. Following that incident, a surprisingly joyful Everton supporter approached him in a local pub, saying that he'd drawn Mick's name in a sweep on the scorer of the first goal and had won £40!

Lyons captained the Blues to the 1977 League Cup Final, in which he scored in the second replay, but it wasn't enough to secure victory over Aston Villa. It was the nearest he came to winning a trophy in his time at Goodison.

Early in 1982 he lost his regular place in the side when Billy Wright was brought into Howard Kendall's constantly changing side to partner Mark Higgins. A recall never came and Lyons severed his ties with the club in August of that year, joining Sheffield Wednesday. A natural choice as captain, he led the Owls to the FA Cup semi-finals in 1982/83, and the following season he was ever present as the club finally won promotion back to the top flight.

In November 1985, Lyons became Grimsby Town's player-coach but was sacked in June 1987 after they were relegated. A month later he rejoined Everton as reserve-team coach. Dismissed following the re-appointment of Howard Kendall, he was appointed first-team coach at Wigan Athletic and then Huddersfield Town. He later accepted a post of coach to the Brunei national team.

# LOU MACARI
Forward
Born 7.6.49, Edinburgh

**LEAGUE RECORD**

|  | A | G |
| --- | --- | --- |
| Manchester United | 311 (18) | 78 |
| Swindon Town | 33 (3) | 3 |

**HONOURS**
Second Division Champions 1974/75
FA Cup 1976/77
24 Scotland caps

Born in Edinburgh of Italian parents, LOU MACARI began his career with Celtic. He had already won two League Championship and two Scottish Cup winners' and losers' medals with the Parkhead club when, in January 1973, he became one of the many Scottish players recruited for Manchester United by Tommy Docherty. Over the years, Macari, who scored on his debut against West Ham United, repaid every penny of the £200,000 United paid Celtic.

A player of great flair, Macari was part of United's attractive side of the mid-1970s. At the end of his first full season at Old Trafford, United were relegated for the first time in thirty-seven years. Macari scored the only goal of the victory over Southampton which secured the club's promotion break to the top flight at the first attempt. Then, after playing in the 1976 FA Cup Final defeat, he had a major hand in victory over Liverpool in the 1977 Final, when his shot was deflected over the line by Jimmy Greenhoff for the winning goal. Two years later he was back at Wembley when United went down 3–2 to Arsenal; but by the mid-1980s, though still an important member of the Reds' squad, he had made way for younger men.

In June 1984, Macari left Old Trafford to join Swindon Town as player-manager. Towards the end of his first season in charge at the County Ground, he was sacked after a row with his assistant, Harry Gregg. He was reinstated six days later and went on to steer the club from the Fourth to the Second Division in two seasons.

In July 1989, Macari left Swindon to take over at West Ham United but lasted only seven months. In January 1990, the FA charged Macari along with Swindon chairman Brian Hillier with unauthorised betting on a Robins match.

Macari returned to management a year later at St Andrew's and took Birmingham to the Leyland Daf Final at Wembley. However, he resigned shortly afterwards, saying the club lacked ambition. He then joined Stoke City, and at the end of his first season took the Potters to the Third Division play-offs, where they lost to Stockport County. They gained some sort of revenge three days later when they beat the Edgeley Park club in the Autoglass Final. In 1992/93, Macari led Stoke to the Second Division title but in November 1993 he left to manage Celtic.

Within four months, the popular Scot was back at Stoke, remaining with the Potters until 1997. He later managed Huddersfield Town but parted company with the club in the summer of 2002. He is now involved in work with the media.

# TERRY McDERMOTT

Midfielder
Born 8.12.51, Kirkby

Though Kirkby-born, TERRY McDERMOTT began his career with homely Bury, for whom he made ninety League appearances before his transfer to Newcastle United.

Although on the losing side in the 1974 FA Cup Final against Liverpool, Terry McDermott had been particularly impressive for the Magpies, and within a matter of months he had been transferred to the Anfield club for a fee of £170,000. But Liverpool won the League Championship and the UEFA Cup in 1975/76 without McDermott's assistance and it seemed only a matter of time before his arrival would be written off as an expensive mistake and he was transferred.

However, Bob Paisley kept faith with him; and the following season saw him firmly established by the spring, playing a memorable role in the run-in which saw the League title and European Cup coming to Anfield (but the FA Cup going to Old Trafford). He was superb and dangerous when running from deep positions and arriving late in the penalty area, where his finishing could be deadly. That campaign saw him score two really outstanding goals. The first came at Maine Road in the FA Cup semi-final against Everton, when he spotted goalkeeper David Lawson off his line and clipped in a beautiful goal. The second was probably the most important goal of his career. It broke the deadlock in the 1977 European Cup Final against Borussia Moenchengladbach in Rome. He ghosted down the inside-right channel to receive Steve Heighway's pass and curl the ball in superb fashion round the German keeper.

It was the following season, when Graeme Souness arrived at Anfield, that McDermott reached his peak. The Scot's style of play allowed the wiry McDermott the freedom he needed to express his talents fully. He covered every blade of grass on the pitch, often acting as a decoy and creating space for his colleagues to exploit. And when in possession, his control and instinctive passing ability allowed him to get the best out of the situation.

> On 17 February 1973 in a Division One match, Newcastle United drew 1–1 with Wolverhampton Wanderers at Molineux. Kenny Hibbitt put Wolves ahead in the first half and his brother Terry equalised for the Magpies after the interval!

**FACT**

In September 1978 he started and finished one of Anfield's best ever goals in the televised 7–0 hammering of Spurs. In 1979/80 he was the club's top scorer with thirteen goals, hitting a hat-trick against Oulu Palloseura, the Finnish Champions, in a 10–1 victory.

In 1980 he became the first man to win awards from the football writers and his fellow players in the same season. He made another valuable contribution in 1981/82, netting fourteen goals in twenty-eight games as Liverpool won the League title and Milk Cup.

On losing a little impetus, he returned to the north-east to team up with Kevin Keegan at Newcastle as the Magpies staged a revival. He later played for Cork City and Apoel, of Cyprus, before returning to St James's Park as Kevin Keegan's successful assistant-manager, a role he held until 1999. McDermott is now involved with work in the media.

## MALCOLM MacDONALD
Forward
Born 7.1.50, Fulham

**LEAGUE RECORD**

| | A | G |
|---|---|---|
| Fulham | 10 (3) | 5 |
| Luton Town | 88 | 49 |
| Newcastle United | 187 | 95 |
| Arsenal | 84 | 42 |

**HONOURS**
Anglo-Italian Cup 1972/73
Texaco Cup 1973/74, 1974/75
14 England caps

Known nationwide as 'Supermac', MALCOLM MACDONALD was a phenomenon of the 1970s.

He began his football career as a full-back with Tonbridge before joining Fulham in August 1968, where manager Bobby Robson switched him to centre-forward. But when Robson left, Macdonald fell out of favour and was transferred to Luton Town for £30,000 in the summer of 1969. In two seasons with the Hatters he averaged well over a goal every other game, scoring forty-nine goals in eighty-eight league outings.

Eventually Newcastle United signed him for a then club record fee of £180,000 in May 1971. On Tyneside, Macdonald became the greatest idol since the days of Jackie Milburn. In one of his first matches for the Magpies, he scored a hat-trick against Liverpool, and he finished each of his five seasons with Newcastle as the leading scorer, racking up a total of 138 goals in 258 games. When the Magpies reached the FA Cup Final in 1974, Macdonald scored in every round of the competition, while the following year he scored five goals in one match for England against Cyprus to equal England's individual scoring record. Consequently the whole of Tyneside was stunned in August 1976 when Macdonald left St James's Park, joining Arsenal for a fee of £333,333.

In his first season at Highbury, he was the First Division's leading scorer with twenty-five goals. In 1977/78 he helped the Gunners to the FA Cup Final, where they lost 1–0 to Ipswich Town. Then, after just four games the following season, he suffered a serious leg injury in a League Cup tie at Rotherham United.

In July 1979, at the age of just 29, Malcolm Macdonald announced his retirement. In a little over two seasons at Highbury, Macdonald had scored fifty-seven goals in 107 League and Cup games.

He returned to Craven Cottage as the club's marketing executive, later being appointed manager. In his first few months in charge, he steered the club clear of relegation to the Fourth Division and in 1981/82 he led the club to promotion to Division two.

The following season he almost took the Cottagers into the top flight, but in March 1984 following revelations about his private life, he left Fulham to run a pub in Worthing. He returned to football as manager of Huddersfield Town before in 1993 moving to Milan, where he was employed in sporting telecommunications. For a period he was also a football agent, assisting in bringing Brazilian star Mirandinha to St James's Park.

Since then he has been on the after-dinner circuit as a speaker, as well as becoming a local-radio commentator and columnist in the north-east.

## LEAGUE RECORD

| | A | G |
|---|---|---|
| York City | 84 | 34 |
| Bournemouth | 197 (1) | 119 |
| Manchester United | 18 | 5 |
| West Ham United | 24 | 5 |
| Norwich City | 112 | 51 |
| Southampton | 86 | 42 |
| Blackpool | 11 (2) | 0 |

**HONOURS**
7 Scotland caps

# TED MacDOUGALL
### Forward
### Born 8.1.47, Inverness

One of the game's most prolific goal-scorers, TED MACDOUGALL began his league career with York City, where he first teamed up successfully with Phil Boyer. Then, in the summer of 1969, he left Bootham Crescent to join Third Division Bournemouth.

Here, on 24 November 1970, in the FA Cup tie against Oxford, he scored six goals; and a year later he netted nine in an 11–1 win over Margate – still the all-time record. Therefore it is not surprising that all the top-flight clubs sought his talents.

Accordingly, in September 1972, amid much publicity, MacDougall signed for Manchester United for a fee of £200,000. Although he had scored 103 goals in 146 first-team outings for the Dean Court club, paying so much money for a Third Division striker was a big gamble for United manager Frank O'Farrell.

In his first few games for United, MacDougall looked out of place in the top flight, although, to be fair to him, he was never given much opportunity afterwards to find his

> **FACT**
> Playing for Rotherham United against Bournemouth on 10 October 1972, Carl Gilbert scored both his team's goals in a 7–2 home defeat – and then had three scored against him after he had become the emergency goalkeeper following an injury to the Millers' keeper.

feet. He had played in just eighteen games for the Old Trafford club when he was transferred to West Ham United – but sadly he was just as unfortunate there.

So in December 1973 MacDougall moved again, this time to Norwich City, where he top-scored for three seasons in a row and was capped seven times by Scotland. MacDougall's best season for the Canaries in terms of goals scored was 1975/76, when his total of twenty-three goals included hat-tricks in two successive home games as Norwich beat Aston Villa 5–3 and Everton 4–2. In August 1976, having scored 66 goals in 138 League and Cup games, MacDougall returned to the south coast with Southampton.

He ended his first season at the Dell as the Saints' top scorer with twenty-three League goals and in 1977/78 netted fourteen as the club won promotion to the First Division. He had scored 47 goals in 101 first-team games for Southampton when in November 1978 he returned to Bournemouth, before ending his long career with his seventh League club, Blackpool.

Later MacDougall, who was the Seasiders' player-coach, briefly came out of retirement in August 1981 to play a few games for Salisbury and later Poole Town and Gosport Borough in 1982. MacDougall, who owned a sports shop in Bournemouth and was later licensee of a pub near Romsey, then emigrated to Canada where he has become a wealthy property developer. Now based in Vancouver, he still follows the fortunes of his beloved Bournemouth.

# ROY McFARLAND
### Central Defender
### Born 5.4.48, Liverpool

**LEAGUE RECORD**

| | A | G |
|---|---|---|
| Tranmere Rovers | 35 | 0 |
| Derby County | 437 (5) | 44 |
| Bradford City | 40 | 1 |

**HONOURS**
League Champions 1971/72, 1974/75,
Second Division Champions 1968/69
Texaco Cup 1971/72
28 England caps

One of the most astute centre-halves since the Second World War, ROY McFARLAND spent only the 1966/67 season with Tranmere Rovers before Brian Clough decided he was the defender to help Derby County out of Division Two. He did just that, playing in all forty-two games and scoring nine goals as the Rams won the Second Division title in 1968/69. He then helped Derby win the League Championship in 1971/72 and again in 1974/75.

Roy McFarland was a polished, classic centre-half who had a good footballing brain, and it didn't take England manager Sir Alf Ramsey long to recognise his qualities. He made his England debut against Malta in 1971 and would have made far more than the twenty-eight international appearances that he did, had it not been for an Achilles tendon injury which he received while playing for his country. Climbing for a high ball – he was remarkably good in the air considering he was only 5ft 11in tall – he landed awkwardly on the pitch. It was a great shame because that injury brought his international career to an early end although he continued to play for Derby County.

After fourteen seasons at the Baseball Ground, he moved to Bradford City and as player-manager led them out of the Fourth Division in 1981/82. Soon after that triumph, he was tempted back to the Baseball Ground as assistant to Peter Taylor, and he continued to play the occasional game. When Taylor left in April 1984, Roy was briefly put in charge until the appointment of Arthur Cox. The new manager persuaded McFarland to stay on as his assistant and together they guided Derby to the Second Division Championship in 1986/87. He stayed at Derby as Cox's assistant until 1993 before taking over the reins himself.

After twenty-six years' service with the club, he left to take charge at Bolton Wanderers in June 1995, with his former Derby County team-mate Colin Todd remaining in the assistant's post. The newly promoted Wanderers won only two games before the turn of the year, and were on course for a swift return to the First Division; this poor run of results culminated in McFarland being dismissed.

After a short spell out of the game, he returned to take charge at Cambridge United and in 1998/99 led the 'U's to promotion to Division Two. He parted company with the club after five years before spending the 2001–02 season in charge of Torquay United.

# DUNCAN McKENZIE
Forward
Born 10.6.50, Grimsby

| LEAGUE RECORD | A | G |
|---|---|---|
| Nottingham Forest | 105 (6) | 41 |
| Mansfield Town | 13 (3) | 10 |
| Leeds United | 64 (2) | 27 |
| Everton | 48 | 14 |
| Chelsea | 15 | 4 |
| Blackburn Rovers | 74 | 16 |

Dazzling showman DUNCAN McKENZIE was one of football's great enigmas. A player of unquestionable brilliance, he turned into a sporting nomad, constantly moving from club to club in a bid to find the right stage for his stunning skills. And at one stage he seemed to spend more time amusing supporters by jumping over cars than actually playing football!

McKenzie began his career with Nottingham Forest but, despite some outstanding performances for the reserve side, he could not produce his top form at first-team level. He was released for loan spells with Mansfield Town, but seven goals in six games in his second spell persuaded the Forest management to give him another chance.

He responded magnificently to top the Second Division scoring charts in 1973/74, ending the season with twenty-eight League and Cup goals. Also that season he was on the England's substitute bench for the Home International Championships, but was not called upon to play.

During his brief reign as Leeds United manager, former Derby County boss Brian Clough spent £240,000 in August 1974 to bring McKenzie to Elland Road. Clough was soon forced to depart but McKenzie stayed to become an idol of the Leeds fans, who loved his style. Despite finishing top scorer in 1975/76, he was sold to Anderlecht in the close season. After netting sixteen goals in thirty games for the Belgian club, a £200,000 move took him to Everton in December 1976.

Shortly after his arrival at Goodison, Everton manager Billy Bingham was sacked and replaced by Gordon Lee. McKenzie and Lee never got on and eventually McKenzie left to play for Chelsea.

Scoring twice in his first three games, he produced glimpses of the audacity that enchanted his admirers; but as the Blues battled against relegation, McKenzie seemed to become a costly irrelevance, and in March 1979 he joined Blackburn Rovers for less than half the £165,000 Chelsea had paid six months earlier.

He later played in the NASL with Tulsa Roughnecks and Chicago Sting. Then, following a spell in the Warrington Sunday League, he went to play in Hong Kong. Later he helped run a football community programme in Liverpool and owned a delicatessen.

Now McKenzie is a noted after-dinner speaker and has written on football for national newspapers and worked as a summariser on radio.

## LEAGUE RECORD

| | A | G |
|---|---|---|
| Leeds United | 140 | 15 |
| Manchester United | 184 | 20 |

## HONOURS
League Champions 1973/74
FA Cup 1982/83
30 Scotland caps

# GORDON McQUEEN
## Central Defender
## Born 26.6.52, Kilwinning

At school, GORDON McQUEEN was a goalkeeper, following in the footsteps of his father Tom, who kept goal for Hibernian, Berwick Rangers, East Fife and Accrington Stanley.

He switched to playing on the wing before settling at centre-half, where his aerial power made him a formidable opponent; and after unsuccessful trials with both Liverpool and Glasgow Rangers he joined St Mirren from Largs Thistle in 1970.

Not long afterwards, Leeds United were looking for a long-term successor to Jack Charlton, and in September 1972 they paid £30,000 to secure his services.

During his time at Elland Road, he developed into an outstanding defender who was first-choice during the Yorkshire club's 1973/74 League Championship-winning season. At the end of that campaign, he won the first of his thirty Scottish caps, in a 2–1 defeat by Belgium in Brussels.

In February 1978 it cost a then British record fee of £495,000 to take him to Manchester United. A month earlier, United manager Dave Sexton had bought McQueen's great friend and Elland Road team-mate Joe Jordan. Eleven days after putting pen to paper, McQueen made his United debut in the toughest of circumstances at Anfield. He went on to appear with the Reds in three Wembley finals: the 1979 FA Cup defeat by Arsenal, the 1983 Milk Cup defeat by Liverpool, and United's two matches against Brighton and Hove Albion which brought them the FA Cup in 1983.

McQueen suffered his fair share of injuries and one of these at Anfield in early 1984 not only kept him out of action for the remainder of the season but also forced him to miss Scotland's appearance in the 1984 World Cup Finals.

In August 1985 he was appointed coach at Seiko FC in Hong Kong, but after just one season he was bedridden and on the danger list with a combination of typhoid fever and septicaemia. After making a full recovery, he took over as manager of Airdrieonians, but in May 1989 he resigned his post because the majority of the Scottish club's players would not play full-time on the contracts offered.

McQueen then ran a greetings-card shop in Paisley and had a spell coaching St Mirren before becoming a match analyser for Scottish television. He later re-entered the English game as reserve-team coach at Middlesbrough but is now again involved with the media.

# WILLIE MADDREN

Central Defender
Born 11.1.51, Billingham
Died 29.8.2000

**LEAGUE RECORD**

|  | A | G |
|---|---|---|
| Middlesbrough | 293 (3) | 19 |

**HONOURS**
Second Division Champions 1973/74
Anglo-Scottish Cup 1975/76

The young WILLIE MADDREN was invited to a trial by Leeds United but a broken ankle prevented him attending and the opportunity passed him by. Subsequently Leeds' loss became Middlesbrough's gain when he signed for the then Ayresome Park club in the summer of 1968.

He was in those days employed initially as a striker and indeed scored on his League debut as Boro went down 3–2 to Bury. (It was an eventful debut, for the young Maddren also broke his nose!)

Over the next few seasons, Maddren was used as a utility man before eventually settling in at centre-back, where he soon established himself as one of the best defenders around – enjoying a seemingly telepathic partnership with captain Stuart Boam at the heart of the Boro defence. Especially outstanding during Middlesbrough's Second Division Championship-winning season of 1973/74, his displays led to his winning five England Under-23 caps. There were many who felt that his blend of aggression and determination, allied to his instinctive reading of the game, would lead to full international honours.

And indeed, that might well have been the case if his career hadn't been ended by a serious knee injury, forcing Maddren to play the last of his 354 League and Cup games at West Bromwich Albion in September 1978.

Aged just twenty-six, Willie Maddren turned to coaching. He started at Hartlepool United but returned to Middlesbrough in 1983, and on Jack Charlton's arrival – back at Ayresome Park after the dismissal of Malcolm Allison – Maddren was promoted to first-team coach. He was then made Middlesbrough's manager for the 1984/85 season on Charlton's recommendation.

In a time of turmoil and mounting debts, Willie Maddren faced an uphill struggle to turn the north-east club's fortunes around, and in February 1986 he was sacked and replaced by Bruce Rioch.

After leaving Middlesbrough, Maddren returned to running a number of sports shops in the area before later working for an insurance firm.

A crowd of over 20,000 attended the Riverside Stadium in August 1996 to see Boro play Inter Milan in a benefit match for Maddren as he battled bravely against motor neurone disease. The former Boro star finally lost his battle on 29 August 2000, aged just forty-nine.

## LEAGUE RECORD

| | A | G |
|---|---|---|
| Plymouth Argyle | 134 (1) | 56 |
| Ipswich Town | 260 | 96 |
| Arsenal | 52 (8) | 14 |
| Portsmouth | 49 (7) | 9 |

## HONOURS
FA Cup 1977/78
UEFA Cup 1980/81
35 England caps

# PAUL MARINER
Forward
Born 22.5.53, Bolton

PAUL MARINER began his career with non-League Chorley before being transferred to Plymouth Argyle for a small fee in July 1973. Within weeks of the start of the 1973/74 season, he had displaced Jimmy Hinch and become recognised as one of the leading forwards in the Third Division; and in 1975/76 his scoring partnership with Billy Rafferty did much to ensure Argyle's promotion to the Second Division. It also attracted the attention of First Division clubs Ipswich Town, West Bromwich Albion and West Ham United, but it was Bobby Robson who made the Devon club an offer they could not refuse in October 1976. With seven goals in ten League games, Mariner had already demonstrated that he could get goals in Division Two as well as Division Three, and Argyle accepted Ipswich's valuation of the player: £220,000 including two Town players, Terry Austin and John Peddelty.

Robson's high opinion of Mariner continued after the former had left Ipswich to become manager of the national team and Mariner was awarded the first of his thirty-five caps some six months after moving to Portman Road.

In his first season with the club, he scored thirteen goals in thirty-one games including a hat-trick in a 4–1 home win over West Ham United. In 1977/78 he was the club's top scorer with twenty-two goals, including another treble in a 6–1 sixth-round FA Cup win at Millwall. He ended the campaign with an FA Cup winners' medal after the Blues had beaten Arsenal 1–0 in the final. He led the scoring charts again in 1978/79 and 1979/80 – in the latter season netting his third hat-trick for the club in a 6–0 win over Manchester United. Although his goal-scoring achievements were fewer over his last three seasons at Portman Road, he had scored 131 goals in 339 games when he signed for Arsenal in February 1984 for a fee of £150,000.

Although hardly in the veteran stage, he had seen his best years; and in August 1986, after scoring seventeen goals in 70 games for the Gunners, he joined Portsmouth. In his first season at Fratton Park he helped the club gain First Division recognition for the first time in almost thirty years.

On leaving Pompey, he had a brief spell as commercial manager of Colchester United before coaching youngsters in Japan as part of a worldwide coaching

organisation masterminded by Charlie Cooke. He also worked for BBC Radio
Suffolk but now lives and works in the United States, coaching young schoolboys
in Phoenix, Arizona.

## LEAGUE RECORD

|  | A | G |
| --- | --- | --- |
| Ipswich Town | 588 (3) | 22 |
| Southampton | 103 | 3 |
| Stoke City | 38 | 0 |

**HONOURS**
FA Cup 1977/78
UEFA Cup 1980/81
Second Division Champions
  1967/68
Texaco Cup 1972/73
42 England caps

# MICK MILLS
Full-Back
Born 4.1.49, Godalming

MICK MILLS began his career with Portsmouth but was released when the Fratton Park club abandoned their youth policy. Ipswich Town snapped him up and it was not long before he made his League debut against Wolverhampton Wanderers, a match the Suffolk club won 5–2. Just over three years later he became the first player in Ipswich history to make 100 league appearances before his twenty-first birthday.

Following Bill Baxter's departure midway through the 1970/71 season, Mills was appointed the club captain and over the next twelve years he led the Tractor Boys by example, earning the nickname 'Captain Fantastic'. In 1973, when his name was already extremely well known around England's big grounds as a full-back or midfield player of non-stop momentum and perception, he was called up for the national side for the first time, when he played against Yugoslavia.

It was then a high personal honour when he captained his country for the first time against Wales at Cardiff in 1978, but his proudest moment was to lead England against the challenge of Switzerland in a World Cup eliminator at Wembley in 1980. An unobtrusive yet inevitable part of the England defensive set-up, Mills won forty-two caps, his last against Spain in 1982.

For Ipswich he was ever present in four successive seasons from 1972/73, appearing in 198 consecutive league games. The highlights of his career were the winning of the FA Cup in 1978, when Arsenal were beaten 1–0, and the defeat of AZ67 Alkmaar in the final of the UEFA Cup in 1980/81.

Mills, who appeared in a club-record 741 first-team games, left Portman Road in November 1982 to join Southampton for a fee of £50,000. He soon fitted in to the Saints style of play and over the next three seasons played in 121 League and Cup games, including being ever present in 1984/85 when the club finished fifth in the First Division.

In 1985 he moved to Stoke City as player-manager but after a few mediocre seasons was replaced by Alan Ball, whom he had recently appointed as his assistant. Mills later managed Colchester United and had a spell as assistant manager at Coventry City. He was also chief scout for Sheffield Wednesday and assistant manager of Birmingham City, but now he provides commentary for BBC Radio Suffolk, and also writes a column in the *Evening Star* twice a week.

Mick Mills, captain of both Ipswich Town and England.

## LEAGUE RECORD

|  | A | G |
|---|---|---|
| Northampton Town | 183 (4) | 28 |
| Liverpool | 453 (2) | 41 |
| Bolton Wanderers | 56 (8) | 3 |

# PHIL NEAL
## Right-Back
## Born 29.2.51, Irchester

## HONOURS

League Champions 1975/76, 1976/77,
  1978/79, 1979/80, 1981/82, 1982/83,
  1983/84
League Cup 1980/81, 1981/82,
  1982/83 1983/84
European Cup 1976/77, 1977/78,
  1980/81, 1983/84
UEFA Cup 1975/76
European Super Cup 1977
50 England caps

PHIL NEAL began his career with Northampton Town and had made 206 appearances for the Cobblers when Bob Paisley bought him for £65,000 in October 1974. He made his Liverpool debut the following month in the Merseyside derby and was ever present from his second appearance for the club in December 1974 until he missed a defeat against Sunderland in October 1983 – a run of 366 consecutive league matches, mostly in the number 2 shirt.

An intelligent, positional player, Neal denied opposing wingers any space. Though he was excellent in defence, his distribution was immaculate. The majority of his goals came from the penalty spot – he hit the clincher in the 1977 European Cup Final from the spot and was on the mark again against AS Roma in 1984. He played in a total of four European Cup Finals, captaining the club in two of them.

His masterly performances at full-back, week in, week out, were an integral part of the Reds' great defensive displays over the years. When he was forced to miss the second leg of a European Cup tie against Odense, it ended a club record 417 consecutive appearances.

Neal won almost every honour going while playing for Liverpool. Picking up seven League Championship medals, he was also on the winning side in four League Cup Finals. He also won a UEFA Cup winners' medal and four European Cup winners' medals – only an FA Cup winners' medal eluded him. And until recently he was the most capped England right-back of all time, with fifty caps to his name, making his last appearance against Denmark in 1983.

Neal succeeded Graeme Souness as skipper for the 1984/85 season but halfway through the following campaign left to join Bolton Wanderers as player-manager. He had made 635 first-team appearances for Liverpool and scored sixty goals.

His first few years in management were eventful – Bolton reached the Freight Rover Trophy Final, were relegated to the Fourth Division, won promotion the following season, and made another visit to Wembley to beat Torquay United in the Sherpa Van Trophy Final. On leaving Burnden Park he had a period of involvement with the England management team before taking charge of Coventry City in November 1993. A year later he took over the reins at Cardiff City before spending a brief spell as caretaker manager of Manchester City.

He now spends his time working in the media.

## LEAGUE RECORD

| | A | G |
|---|---|---|
| Leicester City | 228 | 25 |
| Derby County | 184 (4) | 10 |

## HONOURS
League Champions 1974/75
Second Division Champions
  1970/71
5 England caps

# DAVID NISH
Left-Back/Midfielder
Born 26.9.47, Burton

A teenage prodigy who won numerous England youth honours, DAVID NISH was once chosen as a first-team substitute by Leicester City while he was still at school!

He made a goal-scoring debut for the Foxes against Stoke City in December 1966 and over his first few seasons in Leicester's senior squad exhibited amazing versatility. He first appeared as a creative midfield player and as a defensive wing-half before settling into the side as an attacking left-back. By this time, David Nish's natural ease and cool authority had made him ideal material for the team captaincy and, when the Filbert Street club got to Wembley in 1969, he became the youngest ever FA Cup Final skipper at just twenty-one years of age.

Nish rarely missed a game for Leicester City and amassed ten England Under-23 caps and several Football League representative honours in recognition of his elegant effectiveness. He led Leicester back to the top flight in 1970/71 and looked set for a lengthy career at Filbert Street when reigning champions Derby County came in with a British record fee of £225,000 to take him to the Baseball Ground.

In May 1973, at the end of his first season with the Rams, Nish won the first of five full England caps when he played against Northern Ireland at Anfield, a match in which Martin Chivers scored both England's goals in a 2–1 win.

In 1974/75, Nish was an important member of the Derby County side that won the League Championship, his impressive displays thwarting many an opposition winger. Sadly, after that he began to suffer a series of knee injury problems and decided to leave the Baseball Ground for the less demanding sphere of NASL football when he felt he was slipping from his own high standards of performance.

A testimonial game between the current Rams and their championship-winning predecessors in December 1979 was Derby's fitting farewell to him, but he eventually rejoined his former County team-mates Bruce Rioch and Colin Todd on the coaching staff at Middlesbrough in the summer of 1988.

In July 1991 Nish returned to Filbert Street, some twenty-five years after his initial professional signing, as Youth Development Officer – and additionally assumed coaching responsibility for the youth team during the mid-1990s.

Today he is back at Derby County as the Pride Park club's chief scout.

# PETER NOBLE
Midfielder/Forward
Born 19.8.44, Newcastle

PETER NOBLE's skill and versatility, coupled with his enthusiastic all-action style, endeared him to fans up and down the country and he is still regarded with affection by all who saw him play.

He was playing amateur football on Wearside when he was invited to Blackpool for a trial. After he declined he seemed to have missed his chance of a career in the game, and by the time he turned twenty he was still playing part-time for Consett in the Northern League, while working as a painter and decorator.

Eventually, however, his ability was recognised and in November 1964 he signed for Newcastle United. Here, it took him a couple of seasons to establish himself, but in January 1968 came the chance of a new challenge in Wiltshire.

He was transferred to Swindon Town for £10,000 and in less than a year he had confirmed himself as one of the driving forces behind the Third Division club's resurgence. He played a leading part in Swindon's heroic 3–1 victory over Arsenal in the League Cup Final. Then, after the trophy was secured, it was back to League action and promotion was safely achieved, although the Robins had to be content with second place behind Watford on goal average. In 1970, Noble scored regularly throughout the Anglo-Italian Cup and netted twice in the final before the game was abandoned ten minutes from time thanks to the Italian fans hurling missiles onto the pitch.

In the summer of 1973, Noble left the County Ground to join Burnley, replacing the injured Mick Docherty at right-back. Following the departure of Martin Dobson, Noble was his natural replacement in midfield, and in November 1974 he netted his first hat-trick for the Clarets in a 4–1 defeat of his first club, Newcastle United. In September 1975 he scored all four of Burnley's goals in a 4–4 draw with Norwich City. Later appointed club captain, he led the Clarets to victory in the Anglo-Scottish Cup.

Surprisingly sold to Blackpool in January 1980, he found goals harder to come by; and after the club had been relegated to Division Four, and then had to apply for re-election after finishing in the bottom four, he decided to retire.

These days, one of the most popular players to wear the claret and blue of Burnley is still a very familiar figure in the town – occasionally at Turf Moor but more often at his flourishing sports shop in the town's Market Hall.

# MARTIN O'NEILL
## Midfielder
### Born 1.3.52, Coleraine

**LEAGUE RECORD**

|  | A | G |
| --- | --- | --- |
| Nottingham Forest | 264 (21) | 48 |
| Norwich City | 65 (1) | 12 |
| Manchester City | 12 (1) | 0 |
| Notts County | 63 (1) | 5 |

**HONOURS**

League Champions 1977/78
League Cup 1977/78,
    1978/79
European Cup 1978/79
European Super Cup 1980
Anglo-Scottish Cup 1976/77
64 Northern Ireland caps

Having just won an Irish Cup winners' medal with Distillery in a 3–0 win over Derry City, MARTIN O'NEILL signed for Nottingham Forest in October 1971.

Making his Football League debut as a substitute for the injured John Robertson, O'Neill scored Forest's second goal in a 4–1 win over West Bromwich Albion at the City Ground a month after putting pen to paper. He then faded from the Forest first team and was languishing in the club's reserve side and on the transfer list – but the appointment of Brian Clough as manager seemed to transform O'Neill into a tenacious midfield player and it wasn't long before he was back playing first-team football.

An automatic choice for Northern Ireland throughout his career, winning sixty-four caps, O'Neill won a League Championship medal

> At the end of the 1978/79 season, Nottingham Forest had lost a total of 389 League games while Notts County had drawn 389 times in the same competition.
>
> **FACT**

in 1977/78, two League Cup winners' medals in 1977/78 and 1978/79, and a European Cup winners' medal in 1979/80 as the Reds beat Hamburg SV – having been left out of the Forest side to face Malmo the previous season!

O'Neill had scored sixty-two goals in 371 League and Cup games for Forest, including a spectacular hat-trick in a 6–0 win over Chelsea in March 1979, when he was allowed to leave the City Ground and join Norwich City.

He helped the Canaries avoid relegation in 1981/82 before joining Manchester City. After less than a year at Maine Road, O'Neill rejoined Norwich for a second spell, eventually helping them win promotion to the First Division.

In 1983 he returned to the City of Nottingham – but this time to County, where unfortunately injury ended his career. He then moved into non-League management, first with Grantham Town and then Shepshed Charterhouse before business commitments forced him to quit. Wycombe Wanderers lured him back in February 1990 and he led them into the Football League in 1993. Despite resisting offers from larger clubs, Martin finally returned to one of his former clubs, Norwich City, as manager in June 1995, but left six months later to take over at Leicester City.

He took the Foxes into the Premiership in 1995/96 and kept the club in the top half of the table for the next four seasons before in the summer of 2000 leaving to manage Celtic.

In his first season at Parkhead, O'Neill, who said it took him two and a half seconds to agree to join the Glasgow giants, led the Bhoys to the Scottish Premier League title and to Scottish Cup and League Cup success!

## LEAGUE RECORD

|  | A | G |
|---|---|---|
| Chelsea | 286 (3) | 105 |
| Southampton | 122 (4) | 28 |
| Norwich City | 3 | 0 |

## HONOURS

FA Cup 1969/70, 1975/76
European Cup Winners Cup
  1970/71
4 England caps

# PETER OSGOOD

Forward
Born 20.2.47, Windsor

PETER OSGOOD, a brilliant individualist, graced the English game for over a decade. He scored twice on his Chelsea debut in a League Cup tie against Workington in September 1964, but it was another twelve months before Tommy Docherty gave him an extended first-team run.

It soon became clear that 18-year-old Osgood was very special. He could slice his way through defences with a deceptive swerve, as in a 1966 game at Turf Moor when he beat four Burnley defenders, rounded the keeper and stroked the ball home.

However, in October 1966 Osgood broke his right leg in a clash with Blackpool's Emlyn Hughes, missed the rest of the season and put on two stone which he was never able to lose. It took him a while to regain his confidence but following Ian Hutchinson's arrival he enjoyed the most productive period of his career. In Chelsea's run to the 1970 FA Cup Final, Osgood scored in every round including a hat-trick at Queens Park Rangers and a superb diving header against Leeds United at Old Trafford.

During the 1970-71 season, after a savage eight-week suspension, Osgood scored twice in the second leg of the Cup Winners' Cup quarter-final against Bruges and then found the net in both matches against Real Madrid in Athens to help another trophy on its way to Stamford Bridge.

At the height of his powers Osgood put thousands on the gate and was an automatic choice at Stamford Bridge until he fell out with manager Dave Sexton. Transfer-listed for 'lack of effort', he became involved in a training-ground row after which Sexton walked out and Osgood asked for his cards.

He eventually joined Southampton in 1974 for a fee of £275,000, the first in a line of high-profile stars that Lawrie McMenemy brought to the Dell, but his best efforts couldn't prevent the Saints' relegation to Division Two. Southampton's 1976 defeat of Manchester United brought him another FA Cup Winners' medal but after a loan spell with Norwich City he left to play in the NASL with Philadelphia Furies. He rejoined Chelsea in 1978 but retired after being unable to recapture the old magic.

Since then Osgood has been a Windsor licensee, a coach at holiday camps and a sports promotions manager. He now arranges celebrity golfing breaks and acts as a match day host for Chelsea.

# PHIL PARKES

Goalkeeper
Born 8.8.50, Sedgley

PHIL PARKES began his Football League career with Walsall, but after just fifty-two games for the Saddlers he moved to Queens Park Rangers in the summer of 1970 for a fee of £15,000.

A very formidable figure as a goalkeeper, standing 6ft 3in and weighing over fifteen stone, he stayed at Loftus Road for eight seasons. His goalkeeping helped the club win promotion to the First Division in 1972/73 and then took them to the runners-up spot in the top flight in 1975/76, when they were pipped at the post by Liverpool. In April 1974, Parkes won his one and only full international cap for England when he kept a clean sheet in a goalless draw against Portugal in Lisbon. He also won six England Under-23 caps and played in one game for the England Under-21 side as an over-aged player before he moved to West Ham United in February 1979 for £525,000 – at the time the highest fee ever paid for a goalkeeper.

Parkes made his Hammers debut in a 3–0 home win over Oldham Athletic, the first of 436 first-team appearances in the West Ham goal.

In May 1980 he won an FA Cup winners' medal as the Hammers beat Arsenal 1–0 and he was back at Wembley in March 1981 for the League Cup Final against Liverpool, which the Upton Park club lost after a replay. That season, in addition, he kept twenty-two clean sheets as the club won the Second Division Championship and returned to the top flight. Voted 'Hammer of the Year' in 1980/81, Parkes was ever present in four of his twelve seasons with the club. Injury forced him to miss all but two months of the 1984/85 campaign but the following season he was back to his best, playing in all forty-two matches as the Hammers challenged strongly for the League Championship. After playing in the 6–0 League Cup semi-final defeat at Oldham Athletic, Parkes made way for the Czech international keeper Ludek Miklosko.

Parkes, who had made 344 League appearances for West Ham, exactly the same number he had made for Queens Park Rangers, ended his playing career with three League games for Ipswich Town.

One of a select band of players to have appeared in over 700 League games, he joined Queens Park Rangers as goalkeeping coach in September 1991 but has since returned to Portman Road in a similar capacity.

Probably the finest goalkeeper in West Ham's history, Phil Parkes defended brilliantly against the best attackers in the game.

# STEVE PERRYMAN

Midfielder/Defender
Born 21.12.51, Ealing

## LEAGUE RECORD

| | A | G |
|---|---|---|
| Tottenham Hotspur | 653 (2) | 31 |
| Oxford United | 17 | 0 |
| Brentford | 44 (9) | 0 |

## HONOURS

FA Cup 1980/81, 1981/82
League Cup 1970/71, 1972/73
UEFA Cup 1971/72, 1983/84
1 England cap

Probably the most consistent and loyal player Spurs have ever had, STEVE PERRYMAN holds the record for having appeared in more matches for Spurs than anyone else.

He had already made his Football League debut against Sunderland in September 1969 when he played in the 1970 FA Youth Cup winning side.

Perryman was a member of the Spurs team that won the League Cup in 1970/71 and 1972/73 and the UEFA Cup in 1971/72. In the summer of 1972 he won the first of seventeen England Under-23 caps, against East Germany; and, after he had played in the 1974 UEFA Cup Final, the departure of Martin Peters in March 1975 saw Perryman take over as captain. Though the club were relegated at the end of the 1976/77 season, Perryman led them back to Division One at the first attempt.

Back in the top flight, Perryman switched from playing as a central defender to right-back and it was in this role that he enjoyed some of the highlights of his career, captaining Spurs to their FA Cup victories of 1980/81 and 1981/82 and the 1982 League Cup Final.

In June 1982, Perryman, who won his only full cap as a substitute against Iceland, was voted the Football Writers' Association's Player of the Year.

In the UEFA Cup Final of 1984 he played in the first leg but was forced to sit out the second due to suspension. He still received a medal though, for Ossie Ardilles insisted Perryman should have his, a sign of the respect and esteem in which Perryman was held by his colleagues.

Nobody has won more medals as a Spurs player. Awarded the MBE in the Queen's 1986 Birthday Honours List, he finally left Spurs in March of that year to join Oxford United for £50,000, but two months later he was back in a Spurs shirt playing as a guest in a friendly at Brentford. He later moved to Brentford as player-assistant manager, was promoted to manager, and led the Bees to the sixth round of the FA Cup and Third Division play-offs in 1989. He surprisingly resigned his post at Griffin Park in August 1990 but three months later took over as manager of Watford.

He returned to White Hart Lane, first as assistant manager, then briefly as caretaker manager prior to Gerry Francis taking over the reins. In January 1995 he became assistant to Ossie Ardilles at Shimizu-S-Pulse of Japan's J-League.

## LEIGHTON PHILLIPS
### Central Defender/Midfielder
### Born 25.9.49, Neath

**LEAGUE RECORD**

|  | A | G |
|---|---|---|
| Cardiff City | 169 (11) | 11 |
| Aston Villa | 134 (6) | 4 |
| Swansea City | 97 | 0 |
| Charlton Athletic | 45 | 1 |
| Exeter City | 10 | 0 |

**HONOURS**
League Cup 1974/75, 1976/77
58 Wales caps

LEIGHTON PHILLIPS always harboured the ambition of becoming a professional football player, and after winning Welsh schoolboy international honours he joined the ground staff of Cardiff City.

After working his way through the Ninian Park club's ranks, he made his Football League debut as a substitute in a 2–2 draw at home to Rotherham United in January 1968 – and with his first touch of the ball he scored to draw City level after they had been two goals down.

At Ninian Park, Phillips had plenty of opportunities to show his versatility, appearing as striker, defender and in midfield before succeeding Brian Harris in the role of sweeper. His performances led to him winning Welsh Under-21 and Under-23 caps before he won the first of his fifty-eight full caps, playing against Czechoslovakia in 1971.

In September 1974, after having appeared in 216 first-team games for the Bluebirds, he became dissatisfied at Cardiff's lack of success and left to play for Aston Villa, who paid £80,000 for his services.

Phillips went on to captain the club and to help them win promotion to the First Division and the League Cup in his first season at Villa Park. He also won a League Cup winners' tankard in 1977 when Villa beat Everton, forming an excellent defensive partnership with Chris Nicholl. In fact, it was around this time that Phillips was rated the best covering centre-half in the country. A defender of real pace and determination, Phillips returned to South Wales in November 1978 to join Swansea City, after appearing in 175 League and Cup games for the Villans.

After costing £70,000 to become the Swans' record signing, Phillips went on to help the Vetch Field club win promotion to the Second Division in his first season there. And by the time he left Swansea to join Charlton Athletic in 1981, for a modest £25,000, he had helped the club into the top flight.

His stay at The Valley was brief because the versatile international was beset with injury problems. His last season in the first-class game was 1982/83, when he played as a non-contract player for Exeter City.

Since hanging up his boots, Phillips has worked for Confederation Life Insurance Company in Swansea and is now a senior life underwriter for the company.

# JIM PLATT
Goalkeeper
Born 26.1.52, Ballymoney

LEAGUE RECORD

|  | A | G |
| --- | --- | --- |
| Middlesbrough | 401 | 0 |
| Hartlepool United | 13 | 0 |
| Cardiff City | 4 | 0 |

**HONOURS**
Second Division Champions
  1973/74
Anglo-Scottish Cup 1975/76
23 Northern Ireland caps

The young Irish goalkeeper JIM PLATT had impressed many people while playing for Ballymena and had interested a number of leading clubs, including Liverpool. But his three-week trial at Anfield was followed by the Reds signing Ray Clemence from Scunthorpe United, which scuppered any deal. However, Liverpool's loss proved to be Middlesbrough's gain as Boro manager Stan Anderson paid £7,000 for his services in 1970.

After a homesick first season on the sidelines, Jim Platt took over the number 1 shirt from Willie Whigham just two months into the 1971/72 season. After two

successive defeats in which seven goals had been conceded, Anderson brought in Platt and two clean sheets followed. Platt's form between the posts went on to earn him the club's Player of the Year award at the end of the season.

The following season Platt was ever present. Then, in 1973/74 as Boro won the Second Division Championship, he was outstanding, conceding just twenty-eight goals in forty games, and in doing so keeping twenty-three clean sheets. Platt was then the club's first-choice keeper for the next nine seasons, only occasionally making way for Pat Cuff. But, following the arrival of Jim Stewart for the start of the 1978/79 season, Platt found himself in and out of the Middlesbrough side, having had brief loan spells with Hartlepool United and Cardiff City before reclaiming the number 1 shirt for the season's second half. It wasn't until midway through the 1982/83 campaign that Platt again lost his place. This time the reason was injury, and he was replaced by Kelham O'Hanlon. Once he was fully recovered, however he and a number of other senior players left the club.

Platt, who had made twenty-three full international appearances for Northern Ireland (it would have been many more if it hadn't been for the presence of Pat Jennings) appeared for his country in the 1982 World Cup Finals.

On leaving Ayresome Park he returned to Ballymena as player-manager. After working with a number of other Irish League clubs, he ran his own printing and wholesaling business before returning to the north-east as assistant manager to former Boro team-mate David Hodgson at Darlington. When Hodgson left, Platt took over the reins but was sacked during the early stages of the 1996/97 season. He then had a spell in charge of Gateshead but is now back with Middlesbrough as the club's Football in the Community Officer.

# JOHN PRATT
Midfielder
Born 26.6.48, Hackney

**LEAGUE RECORD**

| | A | G |
| --- | --- | --- |
| Tottenham Hotspur | 307 (24) | 39 |

**HONOURS**
League Cup 1970/71, 1972/73
UEFA Cup 1971/72

Never one to hide, especially in adversity, midfielder JOHN PRATT was a regular choice for Tottenham Hotspur under Bill Nicholson, Terry Neill and Keith Burkinshaw.

He had been a youth-team player with Brentford when recommended to Spurs by the club's former winger Terry Medwin. Pratt was initially a centre-half, but soon switched to wing-half and worked his way through the club's junior and reserve ranks to make his Football League debut in the North London derby against Arsenal in March 1969.

He gradually established himself in the Spurs side, taking over the number 4 shirt when Alan Mullery returned to Fulham. After appearing as a substitute in the first leg of the 1972 UEFA Cup Final, Pratt played in every game of the club's 1972/73 League Cup run, although he only played in twenty minutes of the Final against Norwich City before injury forced him to give way to Ralph Coates. However, he did play in both legs of the following season's UEFA Cup Final.

**FACT**

Playing for Spurs against Burnley in a home match on 5 October 1974, both Mike England and John Pratt put through their own goal during the first half. After the interval, both scored for their own side!

Totally committed to the Spurs cause, John Pratt was a tough, all-action midfielder with a powerful shot, yet there were times when he was never given the credit he deserved. In fact, there were even occasions when he was the butt of the Spurs fans' derision! It was Pratt who worked ceaselessly in midfield to provide the stable ball-winning base which allowed his more talented team-mates to demonstrate their skills.

He was granted a testimonial against Arsenal in May 1978 and remained with the White Hart Lane club until the summer of 1980 when, after scoring 65 goals in 508 appearances, he went to play for Portland Timbers in the NASL.

After three years in North America he returned to White Hart Lane as the club's youth-team coach and served as reserve-team coach and assistant manager until both he and Peter Shreeve were dismissed in April 1986. He then landed a coaching job in Nigeria before returning to work in non-League football circles with Stevenage Borough and Worthing, where he was manager until September 1996.

Living in Chigwell, the former Spurs midfielder has now set up his own window cleaning business.

# KEVIN REEVES

Forward
Born 20.10.57, Burley

**LEAGUE RECORD**

| | A | G |
|---|---|---|
| Bournemouth | 60 (3) | 20 |
| Norwich City | 118 (1) | 37 |
| Manchester City | 129 (1) | 34 |
| Burnley | 20 (1) | 12 |

**HONOURS**

2 England caps

KEVIN REEVES began his career with Bournemouth and was the Cherries' top scorer in his first full season of League football in 1975/76. He joined First Division Norwich City for £50,000 in January 1977, having been tracked by his former manager John Bond, who had himself moved from Dean Court to Carrow Road in 1973, before Reeves had even turned professional.

Under the guidance of Bond, Reeves's career in the top flight blossomed, and, after winning a number of England Under-21 caps, he pulled on a full England shirt for the first time against Bulgaria in the European Championships at Wembley in November 1979.

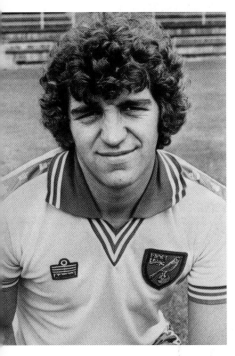

Reeves moved to Manchester City in exchange for a million pounds in March 1980 as Malcolm Allison desperately tried to revive the Blues' flagging fortunes. It didn't work. Exit Malcolm Allison, enter John Bond – to once again team up with Kevin Reeves.

At Maine Road, Reeves once again began to thrive, winning another England cap and top-scoring in each of his first two full seasons with the club. He also scored four goals in City's FA Cup campaign in 1981, including a penalty at Wembley as Spurs edged home by the odd goal in five in a thrilling final replay.

In the summer of 1983, Reeves predictably followed Bond to Burnley and after scoring on his debut at Hull, the signs were that he was still very much a class act. His partnership with Billy Hamilton had yielded thirty-three League and Cup goals when, in January 1984, Reeves suffered the injury that was to end his playing career at the age of twenty-six.

Kevin Reeves then joined the Burnley coaching staff and later coached at non-League level before joining John Bond yet again, this time at Birmingham City.

Soon after Brian Flynn was appointed Wrexham manager in 1989 he brought Kevin Reeves to the Racecourse Ground as his assistant and they guided the Welsh club to promotion to the new Division Two in 1993. The pair stayed with the Robins until 2001 but are now with another Welsh club, Swansea City, doing their utmost to keep the club in the Football League.

**LEAGUE RECORD**

| | A | G |
|---|---|---|
| Arsenal | 391 (6) | 12 |
| Watford | 112 | 1 |

**HONOURS**
League Champions 1970/71
FA Cup 1970/71, 1978/79
Inter Cities Fairs Cup 1969/70
49 Northern Ireland caps

# PAT RICE
Right-Back
Born 17.3.49, Belfast

One of Arsenal's unsung heroes, PAT RICE joined the Gunners as an apprentice in December 1964, turning professional in March 1966. Yet it was only through hard work and determination that the Irishman survived the apprenticeship stage at Highbury.

One of the most loyal players the club has ever had, Rice played in no fewer than five Wembley FA Cup Finals – a record he shares with Joe Hulme, Frank Stapleton and Johnny Giles. He also won forty-nine caps for Northern Ireland and played in 527 League and Cup games for the Gunners – a total bettered only by George Armstrong and David O'Leary.

Despite this, Pat Rice's career had a very unimpressive start. He appeared in just a handful of first-team matches in his first five years at Highbury. However, when Peter Storey was switched from right-back to midfield, Pat Rice was drafted in to the right-back position for the beginning of the 1970/71 season.

> In November 1970, Arsenal carried out tests on their team to determine whether the players were colour-blind. They were not.

**FACT**

In his first full season, he helped Arsenal to the incredible League and FA Cup 'double'. And over the next ten seasons Pat Rice was undoubtedly Arsenal's most consistent player, appearing in every League match during 1971/72, 1975/76 and 1976/77 – becoming one of the few Arsenal players to be an ever-present in three different seasons.

Rice was made Arsenal captain in 1977 and skippered them to three consecutive FA Cup Finals between 1978 and 1980, and the European Cup Winners' Cup Final of 1980.

In November 1980, Rice was transferred to Watford for £10,000, helping the Hornets gain promotion to the First Division in 1981/82 and then finish next season as runners-up to Liverpool.

In 1984, Rice returned to Highbury as youth-team coach and over the next ten years he helped the Gunners to two FA Youth Cup Finals wins and discovered the likes of Andy Cole, Kevin Campbell, Paul Merson, David Rocastle and Michael Thomas, to name but a few.

# PAT RICE

Now the club's assistant manager, having helped the Gunners to the 'double' in 1997/98 and the Premier League title in 2001/02, Pat Rice will forever be remembered for his dedication to the club he loves and supports.

## LEAGUE RECORD

| | A | G |
|---|---|---|
| Wolves | 365 (20) | 144 |
| Derby County | 10 | 2 |

## HONOURS

League Cup 1973/74, 1979/80
Second Division Champions 1976/77
Texaco Cup 1970/71
1 England Cap

One of the most prolific goal-scorers in the history of Wolverhampton Wanderers, JOHN RICHARDS joined the Molineux club straight from school in Warrington in July 1967. Two years later he turned professional and made his League debut in the local derby against West Bromwich Albion in February 1970. His first goal arrived in the Anglo-Italian tournament against Fiorentina in May 1970. Richards, who scored in each of the next twelve campaigns, top-scoring in eight of them, netted his first League goal against Huddersfield Town in September 1970.

Forming a great partnership with Derek Dougan (and later with Bobby Gould, Steve Kindon, Alan Sunderland, Norman Bell, Mel Eves and Andy Gray), it was 1971/72 before he established himself in the Wolves' side, scoring sixteen goals and gaining a UEFA Cup runners-up medal. The following season he was the country's leading scorer with thirty-three League and Cup goals and another three in the Texaco Cup. His total included hat-tricks against Stoke City (home 5–3) and Everton (home 4–2). At the end of that season, he won his only England cap when he played in a 2–1 win over Northern Ireland.

In 1974 he scored the winning goal in the League Cup Final as Wolves beat Manchester City 2–1, and in 1976/77 he helped the club win the Second Division Championship. In 1980 he was a member of the Wolves side that beat Nottingham Forest 1–0 in the League Cup Final.

John Richards is the only Wolves player to have received two benefits – 1982 and 1986 – the second coming three years after he had left the club.

His departure from Molineux came in rather sad circumstances and lots of fans were annoyed at his leaving, this after he had been on loan to Derby County. He joined the Portuguese side Maritimo of Madeira and spent three years there before returning to England to begin working for the Wolverhampton Leisure Services Department.

He later returned to Molineux as the club's managing director.

# BRUCE RIOCH
Midfielder
Born 6.9.47, Aldershot

**LEAGUE RECORD**

|  | A | G |
|---|---|---|
| Luton Town | 148 (1) | 46 |
| Aston Villa | 149 (5) | 34 |
| Derby County | 146 (1) | 38 |
| Everton | 30 | 3 |
| Birmingham City | 3 | 0 |
| Sheffield United | 8 | 1 |
| Torquay United | 64 (7) | 6 |

**HONOURS**
League Champions 1974/75
Third Division Champions 1971/72
Fourth Division Champions 1967/68
24 Scotland caps

The only English-born player to captain Scotland in a full international, BRUCE RIOCH began his career with Luton as an out-and-out attacker before switching to inside-forward. When the Hatters won the Fourth Division Championship in 1967/68, Rioch made his mark as the club's leading scorer with twenty-four goals as they finished five points clear of runners-up Barnsley.

In 1969, Tommy Docherty brought Bruce and his brother Neil to Aston Villa in a combined £100,000 deal. In 1971 Bruce collected a runners-up award in the League Cup Final, and in 1972 he won a Third Division Championship medal. In February 1974, a £200,000 offer took him to Derby County; and in his first full season with the Rams he won a League Championship medal. Shortly afterwards he joined Everton, but his stay at Goodison was brief, and within a year he was back at Derby.

In March 1980 he was released by Derby and joined Seattle Sounders in the NASL, alternating this with the position of player-coach at Torquay United.

Appointed manager of Middlesbrough in February 1986, he guided the club out of a dire financial position, lifting them from the Third to the First Division within two seasons. In 1986/87 he helped the club win promotion to the Second Division as runners-up to Bournemouth and in 1987/88 he took the club into the top flight via the play-offs. But Boro were relegated in 1988/89, and in March 1990, with the club languishing near the foot of the Second Division, Rioch left Ayresome Park.

In less than a month he was in charge of Millwall and in 1990/91 he took the London club to the Second Division play-offs. After their form slumped the following season, however, he resigned to manage Bolton Wanderers. He achieved promotion in his first season when as the Wanderers finished runners-up in Division Two. In 1994/95 he took the club to the League Cup Final and promotion to the Premiership via the play-offs.

In June 1995 Rioch left Bolton to manage Arsenal, but was sacked after fifteen months and joined Queens Park Rangers. After this he managed Norwich City and Wigan Athletic, parting company with the Latics in 2001. He later took temporary charge of Dr Marten's League side Gresley Rovers, but still hopes for a return to Football League management.

## LEAGUE RECORD

| | A | G |
|---|---|---|
| West Bromwich Albion | 504 (2) | 8 |
| Wolves | 107 | 0 |

## HONOURS
Third Division Champions 1988/89
Fourth Division Champions 1987/88
Sherpa Van Trophy 1987/88

# ALISTAIR ROBERTSON
### Central Defender
### Born 9.9.52, Linlithgow

ALLY ROBERTSON was a fine example of the youth policy in operation at West Bromwich Albion in the late 60s and early 70s. He made his league debut in a 2–1 win over Manchester United in October 1969, a month after signing professional forms.

His progress was quick and he went on to win six Scottish youth caps. In 1970, at the age of eighteen, he unfortunately broke his leg playing against Charlton Athletic in a League Cup tie. With grim determination, however, he bounced back as a very consistent performer from there on in. By 1972 he had established himself as first-choice central defender alongside John Wile – a partnership that was to last until Wile's departure in 1983.

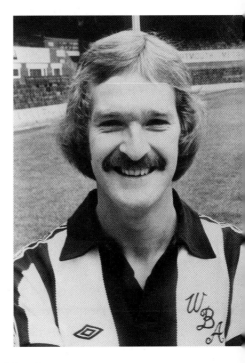

Robertson played in three major Cup semi-finals with Albion – two in the FA Cup – but finished up a loser each time. He also performed on the European circuit, in the UEFA Cup competition. During the five-year period between 1975 and 1980, Ally Robertson missed only seven League games out of a possible 210, and in 1979 he passed Jimmy Dudley's record of 166 consecutive League appearances for the Baggies. But sadly Ally's only triumph with Albion was to help them win promotion from the Second Division in 1975/76.

An uncompromising tackler who certainly made his presence felt among opposition forwards, he had made 760 senior appearances for Albion when in September 1986 he left the Hawthorns on a free transfer to join Wolverhampton Wanderers.

He had an extremely successful three-year stay at Molineux, winning Third and Fourth Division Championship medals, though the highlight probably came at Wembley in 1988 when Wolves carried off the Sherpa Van Trophy in front of an 80,000-plus crowd.

On hanging up his boots, he went into management with non-League Worcester City, although he did still turn out in local charity matches for the Albion All Stars team. In 1991/92 he became manager of Cheltenham Town before returning to the Hawthorns to run the Throstles Club.

# JOHN ROBERTSON
Left-Winger
Born 20.1.53, Uddingston

JOHN ROBERTSON's career had its roots in a nursery team by the name of Drumchapel Amateurs, which also has a claim to fame in producing two other famous Scottish internationals in John Wark and Asa Hartford. Robertson had gained Scottish schoolboy and youth honours before he came south of the border to join Nottingham Forest in May 1970.

However, it wasn't until the arrival of managerial duo Brian Clough and Peter Taylor that Robertson's talent began to be harnessed to its best advantage. The pair encouraged him to do his own thing, be individualistic, hug the touchline, demand the ball at his feet – and waited for him to do the rest.

He gained the first of twenty-eight Scottish caps against Northern Ireland in 1978 and won several honours during Forest's glory years. In particular, he played a prominent part in the club's two remarkable European Cup successes in consecutive years. In the first final, against Swedish champions Malmo in Munich, it was his long cross which winged its way over the goal to the far post for Trevor Francis to head home the game's only goal.

**FACT**

On 9 December 1978, Nottingham Forest came to the end of a run of forty-two consecutive Division One matches in which they had been unbeaten since 20 November 1977.

And twelve months later in Madrid, it was John Robertson's incursion into Hamburg's penalty area, on his right foot, that produced the only goal and kept the top European trophy in this country.

He continued to serve Forest until the summer of 1983, when he left to join Peter Taylor at the Baseball Ground for £135,000, a fee set by an independent tribunal. Unfortunately the winger had to undergo a cartilage operation in his first season at Derby and two years later returned to the City Ground. However, his old magic had deserted him and he moved into non-League football with Corby Town, then Stamford and Grantham.

Most full-backs who figured they knew how to handle the mercurial attacker went into the game assured that Robertson would invariably be at his most dangerous when he cut inside. What they didn't know was exactly when he was going to do it – and that is what made John Robertson lethal.

On hanging up his boots, he became a licensee before working as a sales associate with the Save and Prosper group. He then returned to football as chief scout for former team-mate Martin O'Neill at Wycombe Wanderers. Today he continues to work alongside O'Neill as Celtic's assistant manager.

# JOE ROYLE
Forward
Born 8.4.49, Liverpool

## LEAGUE RECORD

|  | A | G |
| --- | --- | --- |
| Everton | 229 (3) | 102 |
| Manchester City | 98 (1) | 23 |
| Bristol City | 100 (1) | 18 |
| Norwich City | 40 (2) | 9 |

## HONOURS
League Champions 1969/70
League Cup 1975/76
Anglo-Scottish Cup 1977/78
6 England caps

If JOE ROYLE had followed his father's trade, he would have entertained crowds in a very different way, for Joe's father was a musician with a local trio.

Royle made his debut for Everton against Blackpool in January 1966, at the tender age of sixteen years and 282 days, becoming the youngest ever player to represent the Blues until his record was beaten in 2002 by Wayne Rooney. Even at that age, Royle was stocky and powerful and had all the energy, confidence and skill of youth. It was after this game – Everton lost 2–0 – that manager Harry Catterick was attacked by the fans. Young Joe made only one more first-team appearance that season: at Leeds, where the Blues were beaten again, this time 4–1.

It was towards the end of the 1966/67 season when Royle was given another chance. He grabbed it – hitting two goals in a 3–1 win over Chelsea. That was the first time he had appeared before his own fans, and it was a display that banished the bitter Blackpool memory. He went on to play in four games towards the end of the campaign, netting three goals.

Within four years, Royle had packed a wealth of experience into his sizeable frame and earned himself a reputation as one of Everton's finest post-war strikers and a fitting successor to the traditions of Dixie Dean and Tommy Lawton.

Royle was the Blues' leading marksman in the 1968/69 season with twenty-two goals, and again the following season with twenty-three as Everton won the League Championship. He was one of the deadliest strikers of a ball in the top flight and had an ability to head the ball not seen at Goodison since the days of Dixie Dean. His career, however, was dogged by injury and he eventually moved to Manchester City. It was a little surprising that Everton boss Billy Bingham should let him go at the time he did, however, for the Blues were desperately short of goal-scoring talent. Royle was one of the most prolific goal-scorers since the war, scoring 119 goals in 272 games for Everton. He also won six international caps, the first coming against Malta in 1971.

He scored 31 goals in 117 games for the Maine Road club before moving on to Bristol City and later Norwich City, where his playing career came to a premature end because of injury.

Entering management with Oldham Athletic, he combined integrity, humour and sound judgement as the Latics won promotion from the Second Division and reached the League Cup Final and FA Cup semi-final. In November 1994 he returned to Goodison as manager, but after clashes with the chairman over transfer deals, Royle quit the club by mutual consent. He then took Manchester City into the Premiership after successive promotions but lost his job following the club's relegation in 2000/01. Royle is now manager of First Division Ipswich Town.

# PETER SHILTON

Goalkeeper
Born 18.9.49, Leicester

Undoubtedly one of the greatest goalkeepers of the modern era, PETER SHILTON holds the English appearance record with 125 caps, and it was only a few years ago that he was surpassed as the most capped goalkeeper in the world by the Swedish number 1 Thomas Ravelli.

A schoolboy prodigy, helping Leicester Boys to their 1965 Trophy win, he became Leicester City's youngest ever First Division debutant at the age of sixteen, when, characteristically, he kept a clean sheet. He continued to make great progress to the point where he put Leicester boss Matt Gillies under pressure to play him at the expense of England international Gordon Banks or let him go. In the end, Gillies sold Banks and Shilton started to accumulate appearances and records. During the club's 1970/71 Second Division Championship-winning season, Shilton helped create the club's best-ever defensive record with twenty-three clean sheets. He was rarely out of the public eye – his adoption of an all-white playing kit and his long-distance scoring success at Southampton at various times assured that!

In November 1974, after appearing in 339 games for the Foxes, he joined Stoke City for £325,000, then a world record fee for a goalkeeper. When the Potters dropped into Division Two, Shilton was the subject of a typically shrewd piece of business by Brian Clough, who paid £240,000 for his services.

In terms of honours, he enjoyed his best years with Nottingham Forest, being selected PFA Player of the Year in 1978 plus gaining a League Championship medal, a League Cup winners' medal and two European Cup winners' medals. He left Forest in August 1982 after playing in twenty-two games to join Southampton for £300,000.

In 1983/84 he was ever present, keeping eighteen clean sheets as the Saints ended the campaign as First Division runners-up to Liverpool. While at the Dell, he also became the most capped England keeper of all time, skippered the national side, and earned the MBE. Then, following a big-money transfer to Derby County in June 1987, he set about creating a further series of career landmarks: he passed Terry Paine's all-time record for the highest number of League appearances and overtook Bobby Moore's record haul of England caps.

After retiring from the international scene, he was upgraded to the OBE in 1991 and later took the plunge into management with Plymouth Argyle. Unable to juggle the pressures of a relegation fight with those of his well-publicised personal financial difficulties, he resigned after being suspended by his chairman.

He then amazingly came back as a player, first with Bolton Wanderers and then West Ham United before joining Leyton Orient where, four days before Christmas 1996, he made his 1000th League appearance and was given a special award to mark the achievement by the Football Association.

The former England keeper now earns a living as an after-dinner speaker.

# DENNIS SMITH

Central Defender
Born 19.11.47, Stoke-on-Trent

**LEAGUE RECORD**

|  | A | G |
| --- | --- | --- |
| Stoke City | 406 (1) | 29 |
| York City | 37 | 5 |

**HONOURS**
League Cup 1971/ 72

Idolised by the Stoke public for his total commitment, DENNIS SMITH overcame countless injuries and broken bones to establish himself in the number 5 shirt, which he was to make his own.

Smith made his Stoke City debut against Arsenal at Highbury in September 1968 and it wasn't long before he won a regular place alongside Alan Bloor at the heart of the Stoke defence. Although he was not the most cultured of defenders, there were, nonetheless, not too many strikers who enjoyed playing against him. There are a number of stories about Dennis Smith's playing days that will live on in the club's football histories and legends.

**FACT**

Birmingham City were the first club to be involved in a penalty shoot-out in an FA Cup game. On 5 August 1972 at St Andrew's against Stoke City (in a play-off for third place held over from the previous season), Birmingham won 4–3 after a goalless draw.

There was the occasion when the club's trainer came on to the pitch to be told by Dennis that he thought he had broken his leg. The trainer replied that he should know, as he had broken it enough in the past! And, on 23 February 1974, Smith scored the winning goal against Leeds United, as Stoke came from two goals down to win 3–2 and end the Yorkshire side's record-breaking run of games without defeat.

Though he represented the Football League XI, a full international cap eluded him. However, he did win a League Cup winners' medal in 1972 as Stoke beat Chelsea 2–1 in the Wembley final.

A man who would run through a brick wall for Stoke City, Dennis Smith, who scored 41 goals in 482 first-team games, joined the club's coaching staff towards the end of his stay at the Victoria Ground and earned a deserved testimonial.

He was appointed York City player-manager in May 1982 and in 1983/84 plotted their Fourth Division title success and consecutive FA Cup runs.

In June 1987 he took charge of Sunderland and led them from the Third Division to the First in three years. While he was at Roker Park, there was a chance for him to return to the manager's desk at Stoke and lead the club back to the top flight, but he chose to stay in the north-east until March 1992 when he replaced Jimmy Lumsden at Bristol City. He guided them to Second Division safety but after a poor start to the 1992/93 campaign, he parted company with the club, becoming manager of Oxford United in September 1993.

Masterminding the club's 1995/96 promotion success, Smith left at the end of the following season to take charge of West Bromwich Albion, before returning for a brief spell in 2000. The former tough-tackling defender is now manager of Wrexham and last season led the Welsh club to promotion to Division Two.

# GRAEME SOUNESS
Midfielder
Born 6.5.53, Edinburgh

Throughout his career, GRAEME SOUNESS has exhibited a fierce desire to succeed, but with established midfielders of the quality of Mullery, Peters and Perryman at White Hart Lane, his first stamping ground, the young Souness grew frustrated. After playing for Montreal Olympic in the NASL in the summer of 1972, he walked out on the club before Spurs released him to move to Middlesbrough for £32,000.

At the end of his first season at Ayresome Park, Middlesbrough were promoted to Division One, and during his stay in the north-east Souness developed into one of the game's most influential performers of modern times.

It was Bob Paisley who brought Souness to Liverpool in January 1978 for £352,000 – then a record deal between Football League clubs. His move to Liverpool to team up with Kenny Dalglish was the foundation stone of the club's success over the next decade. The two dovetailed perfectly and Souness provided the pass for Dalglish to score the winning goal against Bruges in the 1978 European Cup Final.

His displays in the European Cup campaign of 1980/81 were particularly eye-catching, with his sense of awareness and ability to rip open the hearts of defences with long, telling passes. He also hit two hat-tricks in the early stages of the competition, as Liverpool beat Oulu Palloseura of Finland 10–1 and CSKA Sofia of Bulgaria 5–1 in the Anfield legs. But of the goals he scored for Liverpool, none was perhaps more valuable than the one that beat Everton in the 1984 League Cup Final replay. Replacing Phil Thompson as captain, he led the Reds to three successive League titles and League Cups and one European Cup, becoming the most successful skipper in the club's history.

In June 1984 he moved to Sampdoria in Italy for £650,000. Two quiet seasons were followed by his surprise appointment as player-manager at Ibrox in 1986. There, in his first game for Rangers, he was sent off! However, by the end of his first season, the club had won the Scottish League and the Skol Cup and reached the final of the Scottish Cup. Then in 1989/90 they won the Scottish League title again and in 1990/91 they won the Skol Cup.

In April 1991 Souness left Ibrox to replace former Anfield team-mate Kenny Dalglish as manager of Liverpool. In his first season Souness made many expensive changes and, after the shock of undergoing major heart surgery, led the Reds to the one trophy he had failed to capture as a player, the FA Cup. In January 1994, Souness resigned his post and spent a season in Turkey as manager of Galatasaray, but was sacked after winning the Championship. In July 1996 he was appointed manager of Southampton but resigned after a season following a disagreement about money for new players. After a spell managing Serie 'B' club Torino, he took charge of Blackburn Rovers and, having led them to promotion to the Premiership in 2000/01, he saw them win the following season's League Cup at the Millennium Stadium.

# ALAN STEVENSON
Goalkeeper
Born 6.11.50, Staveley

**LEAGUE RECORD**

| | A | G |
|---|---|---|
| Chesterfield | 104 | 0 |
| Burnley | 438 | 0 |
| Rotherham United | 24 | 0 |
| Hartlepool United | 35 | 0 |

**HONOURS**
Third Division Champions 1981/82
Fourth Division Champions 1969/70
Anglo-Scottish Cup 1978/79

As well as football, the teenage ALAN STEVENSON excelled at cricket and was invited for trials with Derbyshire. He was also an outstanding table tennis player and represented his county on numerous occasions. However, football was the first love of this talented all-rounder and he signed for his local club Chesterfield, initially as an amateur after some outstanding displays for the town's schools side.

He made his Football League debut for the Spireites in October 1969 and immediately became the club's first-choice keeper. After helping Chesterfield win the Fourth Division Championship in 1970, his name was linked with a number of top clubs, and in January 1972 Burnley manager Jimmy Adamson paid £50,000 for his services.

Stevenson was already being strongly tipped to win international honours when he signed for the Clarets but, though he went on to win eleven Under-23 caps, he never quite fulfilled his ambitions to represent his country at full international level. He did make the full squad for England's match against Portugal in Lisbon in April 1974, Sir Alf Ramsey's last game as England manager, but remained on the bench as Phil Parkes won his only cap.

He was ever present when Burnley won the Second Division Championship in 1972/73, and his sheer consistency, week in, week out, coupled with breathtaking saves when needed, helped the club have two successful seasons in the top flight. Though he lost his place to Gerry Peyton midway through the 1975/76 season, following a spell of indifferent form, he regained the number 1 jersey the following season. Though the late 1970s were difficult years for Burnley, Stevenson was consistency itself and helped the club win the Third Division Championship in 1981/82. However, at the end of the following season, Stevenson, who had made 543 appearances in his eleven years at Turf Moor, was released.

After a season at Rotherham he joined Hartlepool, initially on loan, and in 1984/85, his last season of League football, he was also appointed the club's commercial manager.

**FACT**

In 1970/71, Lancashire suffered badly from relegation. Burnley and Blackpool went down from Division One to Division Two, Blackburn Rovers and Bolton Wanderers went from Two to Three and Bury from Three to Four. Barrow had to seek re-election after finishing bottom of Division Four.

After his playing days were over he stayed at the Victoria Ground for a time before continuing his successful marketing activities with Middlesbrough, West Bromwich Albion and finally Huddersfield Town, where he remained until 1998.

# ALAN SUNDERLAND

Forward/Midfielder
Born 1.7.53, Mexborough

**LEAGUE RECORD**

|  | A | G |
| --- | --- | --- |
| Wolves | 139 (19) | 30 |
| Arsenal | 204 (2) | 55 |
| Ipswich Town | 51 (7) | 11 |

**HONOURS**
FA Cup 1978/79
League Cup 1973/74
Second Division Champions
  1976/77
1 England cap

Remembered by Arsenal fans as the man who scored the winning goal in the final minute of the 1979 FA Cup Final against Manchester United, ALAN SUNDERLAND began his career with Wolverhampton Wanderers.

During his seven seasons at Molineux, he appeared in a number of different positions, having made his debut in midfield in a 2–1 home win over Manchester City in August 1971. That season he helped Wolves reach the UEFA Cup Final, where they lost over two legs to Tottenham Hotspur. It was 1973/74 before he won a regular place in the Wolves side, going on to appear in the League Cup Final as the Molineux club beat Manchester City 2–1. During Wolves' relegation season of 1975/76, he was used as an emergency right-back, but when the club won the Second Division Championship the following season, he had reverted to the forward line and scored sixteen goals in forty-one games, including a hat-trick in a 4–0 home win over Carlisle United.

In November 1977, Sunderland, who had scored thirty-five goals in 198 games, joined Arsenal for £220,000. He immediately established himself in the Gunners side and ended his first season by playing in the FA Cup Final against Ipswich Town. In 1978/79 he scored six goals in Arsenal's victorious FA Cup campaign and won an England Under-21 cap to add to the Under-23 cap he had won at Wolves.

In 1979/80 he scored twenty-eight first-team goals, forming a prolific goal-scoring partnership with Frank Stapleton. He helped the Gunners to both the FA Cup and European Cup Winners' Cup Finals of that season as well as winning an England cap against Australia. He continued to find the net on a regular basis and was the club's leading scorer in 1981/82. Injuries and the signing of Charlie Nicholas then restricted his first-team appearances; and when Paul Mariner joined the club in February 1984, Alan Sunderland moved to Ipswich Town on loan, the move later being made permanent.

He later played in Ireland for Derry City before ending his involvement with the game. He then ran a property rental company and sold insurance before becoming licensee of the Halberd Inn just outside Ipswich.

# BRIAN TALBOT
Midfielder
Born 21.7.53, Ipswich

**LEAGUE RECORD**

|  | A | G |
|---|---|---|
| Ipswich Town | 177 | 25 |
| Arsenal | 245 (9) | 40 |
| Watford | 46 (2) | 8 |
| Stoke City | 51 (3) | 5 |
| West Brom. Albion | 66 (8) | 5 |
| Fulham | 5 | 1 |
| Aldershot | 11 | 0 |

**HONOURS**
FA Cup 1977/78, 1978/79
Texaco Cup 1972/73
6 England caps

All-action midfielder BRIAN TALBOT began his career with home-town club Ipswich Town. After turning professional in August 1972, he had a two-year loan spell with Toronto Metros before returning to Portman Road to make his League debut at Burnley in February 1974.

Talbot spent seven seasons at Portman Road, playing in 227 first-team games, and won five England caps, the first against Northern Ireland in 1977. He was also a member of the Town side that beat Arsenal 1–0 in the FA Cup Final of 1978.

In January 1979, Talbot was transferred to Arsenal for a then club record fee of £450,000. At the end of that season, he was a member of the Gunners' FA Cup-winning team against Manchester United and thus became the only player ever to play for different cup-winning teams in successive seasons – a distinction he still holds.

In 1979/80, Talbot created an Arsenal club record when he appeared in all of the Gunners' seventy first-team games (the most first-team games played by an Arsenal player in one season). Also that season he played in both losing major finals: in the FA Cup against West Ham United and in the European Cup Winners' Cup against Valencia. His commitment to the North London club was so great that in the match against the Hammers, when the final whistle blew, he collapsed with exhaustion. However, he recovered to play in England's tour of Australasia during the summer of 1980, where he won his sixth and final England cap.

Talbot's play was built around his great stamina. He was the workhorse, the dynamo and the driving force behind Arsenal's midfield, playing in a staggering 380 games for the club in his six seasons at Highbury.

However, following the arrival of Steve Williams from Southampton, Talbot realised his Arsenal days were over and he joined Watford for £150,000 in June 1985. Talbot later played for Stoke City, West Bromwich Albion and Fulham. After serving as chairman of the PFA, he went into management with west Bromwich Albion and then Aldershot before moving overseas to take charge of Hibernians in Malta.

Since 1997, Brian Talbot has been manager of Rushden and Diamonds, helping them to achieve Football League status in 2001 and promotion to Division Two in 2003.

# DAVE THOMAS
Winger
Born 5.10.50, Kirkby-in-Ashfield

**LEAGUE RECORD**

| | A | G |
|---|---|---|
| Burnley | 153 (4) | 19 |
| Queens Park Rangers | 181 (1) | 28 |
| Everton | 71 | 4 |
| Wolves | 10 | 0 |
| Middlesbrough | 13 | 1 |
| Portsmouth | 24 (6) | 0 |

**HONOURS**
Third Division Champions 1982/83
8 England caps

Winger DAVE THOMAS began his career with Burnley where, following an injury to Ralph Coates, he was handed the number 11 shirt for his Division One debut against Everton on 13 May 1967. At sixteen years and 220 days, he was Burnley's youngest ever First Division player and the club's second-youngest debutant of all time, just 46 days older than the legendary Tommy Lawton.

Following Willie Morgan's transfer to Manchester United, he won a regular first-team place during 1968/69. In October of that season, Thomas excelled in Burnley's 5–1 thrashing of Leeds United, whose manager Don Revie enthused that the youngster was the finest in Britain and possibly all Europe. After international appearances at youth level, Thomas won his first England Under-23 cap when still six months short of his twentieth birthday.

Following Burnley's relegation from the top flight in 1971, Thomas lost some of his sparkle and was transferred to Queens Park Rangers for £165,000. He repaid the Londoners' faith in him by inspiring them to promotion to the top flight in 1973 as runners-up to Burnley! Constantly on the top of his form at Loftus Road, he won the first of eight full England caps in October 1974, his first touch creating a goal for Mick Channon in a 3–0 defeat of Czechoslovakia. In 1975/76, Thomas missed just one game as Rangers finished runners-up to Liverpool, just a point behind the Merseysiders.

Following another year in London, Thomas returned to the north-west with Everton, helping them finish third in Division One in 1978. In 1979 he joined Wolverhampton Wanderers but the move didn't work out and he went to play in the NASL for Vancouver Whitecaps. After a short spell with Middlesbrough, he joined Portsmouth, helping Pompey to the Third Division Championship.

He later became the south-coast club's youth-team coach before moving to a similar position with Brentford. After dropping out of football, he moved to Sussex and set himself up as a landscape gardener.

# PHIL THOMPSON
## Central Defender
### Born 21.1.54, Liverpool

**LEAGUE RECORD**

|  | A | G |
|---|---|---|
| Liverpool | 337 (3) | 7 |
| Sheffield United | 36 (1) | 0 |

**HONOURS**
League Champions 1972/73, 1975/76,
    1976/77, 1978/79, 1979/80,
    1981/82
FA Cup 1973/74
League Cup 1980/81,
    1981/82
European Cup 1976/77, 1977/78,
    1980/81
UEFA Cup 1972/73, 1975/76
European Super Cup 1977
42 England caps

As a youngster, PHIL THOMPSON stood on the Kop to cheer his favourites, so it was a dream come true when he actually signed on at Anfield. Bill Shankly used to say about Thompson, 'He's tossed up with a sparrow for legs and lost.' And, indeed, Thompson's frail-looking frame gave the impression that he wouldn't make a top-class defender because he lacked the necessary physical attributes. But this couldn't have been further from the truth, for Phil's determination and skill earned him the captaincy of both Liverpool and England.

Originally a midfielder, Thompson made his debut as a substitute for the Reds against Manchester United at Old Trafford in April 1972. The following season he played in enough matches, in a variety of positions, to qualify for a League Championship medal. Bill Shankly then spotted potential in Thompson in an unlikely role. With regular centre-back Larry Lloyd injured, it was Thompson that Shankly turned to as Emlyn Hughes's partner.

In the 1974 FA Cup Final, Thompson completely shackled the Newcastle United and England centre-forward Malcolm Macdonald as Liverpool ran out 3–0 winners in one of the most one-sided post-war finals.

The Thompson–Hughes combination grew in authority at the heart of the Reds' defence. It was a partnership that played a great part in Liverpool's success as the trophies piled up during the second half of the 1970s.

Thompson was a great reader of the game, often playing his way out of trouble in European style, keeping the ball and setting up attacks with superb distribution. Liverpool often attacked en masse and it was Thompson who was left at the back ready to deal with any possible breakaways – he was probably the most accomplished British defender in a one-to-one situation. Having said that, it was Phil Thompson who was involved in that televised and much debated League Cup Final replay of 1977/78 against Nottingham Forest. When John O'Hare broke away, Thompson chased after him and brought him down just outside the area; and, despite Liverpool's strong protests, the referee awarded a penalty and John Robertson tucked it away.

When Emlyn Hughes lost his place to Alan Hansen, it was Phil Thompson who took over the captaincy. He was a great motivator, inspiring his team-mates to new heights. As captain, he led the Reds to two League Championships and

European Cup success over Real Madrid in 1981. He played forty-two times for England and had a stint as captain.

After Graeme Souness then became captain, Thompson won two further League Championship medals. Thompson's career on Merseyside came to an end in 1985 after being hit by a spate of injuries. He moved on to Sheffield United but wasn't away for long, for eighteen months later he was invited back to Anfield as a member of the coaching staff.

Later a pundit for Sky TV, Thompson, one of the Kop's greatest sons, is now back at Anfield as assistant manager to Gerard Houllier.

## LEAGUE RECORD

| | A | G |
|---|---|---|
| Sunderland | 170 (3) | 3 |
| Derby County | 293 | 6 |
| Everton | 32 | 1 |
| Birmingham City | 92 (1) | 0 |
| Nottingham Forest | 36 | 0 |
| Oxford United | 12 | 0 |
| Luton Town | 2 | 0 |

## HONOURS

League Champions 1971/72, 1974/75
Third Division Champions 1983/84
Texaco Cup 1971/72
27 England caps

# COLIN TODD

Central Defender
Born 12.12.48, Chester-le-Street

COLIN TODD was that rare footballer – a defender who could excite spectators. One of the classiest defenders English football has ever produced, Todd had the ability to send a cross-field pass perhaps fifty to sixty yards to the feet of a team-mate.

He began his career with Sunderland, making his League debut for the Wearsiders against Sheffield United in October 1966. He missed very few games in his five seasons at Roker Park before joining Derby County in February 1973 for £180,000 – then a record fee for a defender.

He was at the time England Under-23 captain, but it wasn't long before he won the first of twenty-seven full caps, when in May 1972 he played against Northern Ireland. At the Baseball Ground, Todd won two League Championship medals and played in the European Cup. His second League Championship success in 1974/75 was probably his greatest season, in which he rarely made an error. At the end of that campaign, he was voted the PFA's Footballer of the Year.

In September 1978, Everton beat off Southampton and signed the 29-year-old perfectionist for £300,000. He brought a calm assurance to an inconsistent side before being laid low by a mystery stomach complaint. After falling out with the Blues boss Gordon Lee, Todd was transferred to Birmingham City for £275,000. He helped the St Andrew's club gain promotion to the First Division in 1979/80 before rejoining Brian Clough at Nottingham Forest for £70,000. Todd ended a fine playing career with Oxford United, the Manor Ground club winning the Third Division title in 1983/84. When he retired at the end of the following season, Todd had played in a total of 749 League and Cup games for his seven clubs.

After managing Whitley Bay for a while, he was assistant manager to Bruce Rioch at Middlesbrough, eventually succeeding him as manager. He later became assistant manager to Rioch again, this time at Bolton Wanderers, where he played an important role in the club's promotion to the Premier League and in the Wanderers' Cup exploits which culminated in them reaching the League Cup Final at Wembley in 1995. When Rioch left, Todd took over the reins and although he couldn't prevent them being relegated, led them back to the Premiership as champions in 1996/97. Todd stayed at the Reebok Stadium until September 1999 when, following the sale of Per Frandsen to Blackburn Rovers, he walked away from the club.

Since then, Todd has managed Swindon Town before quitting to become Jim Smith's assistant at Derby County. Todd later replaced the 'Bald Eagle' as manager but, after just 98 days in charge, his reign came to an end and he is now working as a football agent.

## JOHN TOSHACK
Forward
Born 22.3.49, Cardiff

### LEAGUE RECORD

|  | A | G |
| --- | --- | --- |
| Cardiff City | 159 (3) | 75 |
| Liverpool | 169 (3) | 74 |
| Swansea City | 58 (5) | 24 |

### HONOURS

League Champions 1972/73, 1975/76 1976/77
FA Cup 1973/74
European Cup 1976/77
UEFA Cup 1972/73, 1975/76
European Super Cup 1977
40 Wales caps

JOHN TOSHACK began his career with his home-town team, Cardiff City, breaking into the Bluebirds' first team in 1965/66, when at the age of sixteen years and 236 days he scored the final goal in a 3–1 win over Leyton Orient.

Toshack continued to find the net over the next few seasons and in 1968/69 was the Second Division's leading scorer. By the time he left Ninian Park to sign for Liverpool for £110,000 in November 1970, he had scored 100 goals in 203 games and was already a Welsh international, having been capped against Scotland in 1969. He won over the Reds' fans immediately, for in the derby game with Everton, he turned things round after Liverpool had gone 2–0 down. He scored Liverpool's equalising goal, climbing high above Brian Labone to power in a ferocious header, and then nodded down an Alec Lindsay cross for full-back Chris Lawler to clinch a 3–2 victory.

Toshack's most prolific season was 1975/76, when he scored twenty-three goals, including three hat-tricks, as Liverpool won the League Championship and the UEFA Cup. In his seven seasons at Liverpool, he scored ninety-five goals in 236 games. It was his heading ability that won him the most of his accolades, gaining a reputation for scoring with far-post headers; though, to be fair, he also possessed a deceptively neat touch on the ground. The partnership he established with Kevin Keegan made the pair of them the most feared attacking force in the First Division. They were almost impossible to contain, some pressmen claiming that they had some kind of telepathic understanding!

For most of his Anfield career, Toshack was dogged by a nagging thigh injury and indeed only once did he exceed thirty League games in a season. In March 1978, even though a host of English and foreign clubs were trying to sign him, Liverpool let him go on a free transfer to become player-manager of Swansea City.

He scored on his debut for the Swans, helping the club clinch third place and promotion to Division Three. In a three-year spell with Toshack as their manager, Swansea climbed from the Fourth to the First Division – a feat unrivalled in Football League history. Sadly, though, it all went wrong for Toshack as the Welsh club had debts of more than £1 million from his spending in the transfer market, and the team began to disintegrate at an alarming rate. He resigned with

eighteen months of his contract still to run and asked for no compensation. (He then returned eight weeks later but couldn't halt the slide and was sacked.)

After managing Sporting Lisbon, he bounced back in 1986 as manager of Real Sociedad, winning the Spanish Cup by beating Athletico Madrid in his first season. He then took charge of mighty Real Madrid, winning the Championship in his first season. Despite this, the club sacked him shortly afterwards and in 1991 he returned to Real Sociedad as general manager.

In March 1994, a spell as Welsh national team manager lasted a mere forty-four days and one game before he returned to Spain to take over at Deportivo La Coruna. He later had a second spell in charge of Real Madrid but was sacked in November 1999 halfway through his contract.

## LEAGUE RECORD

|  | A | G |
|---|---|---|
| Sunderland | 173 (5) | 46 |
| Manchester City | 216 (8) | 86 |
| Stoke City | 2 (1) | 0 |
| Burnley | 8 (7) | 5 |

**HONOURS**
FA Cup 1972/73
League Cup 1975/76
6 England caps

# DENNIS TUEART
### Winger
### Born 27.11.49, Newcastle

After earning rave reviews for Newcastle Schoolboys, DENNIS TUEART slipped through the St James' Park net when Sunderland signed him in 1966. He was a regular in the team relegated from the top flight in 1970 and the rest of his Roker Park career was spent in the Second Division.

The highlight undoubtedly was the Wearsiders' memorable victory over the mighty Leeds United in the FA Cup Final of 1973, one of the biggest cup upsets of all time.

During the club's first ever European campaign, in the Cup Winners' Cup of 1973/74, Tueart scored in both legs of the first round against Vasas Budapest, both of which were won by the north-east club. However, after Sunderland's exit at the hands of Sporting Lisbon, Tueart was transferred to Manchester City in March 1974 for £275,000, then a record fee for both clubs.

Tueart was approaching the peak of his form and, just days after joining the Maine Road club, his fast direct wing play brought international recognition for the first time. He was selected for the Football League and scored in the 5–0 demolition of the Scottish League in a match staged at his new home ground, Maine Road. In December 1974 he was chosen as an over-age player in England's Under-23 side to meet Scotland at Pittodrie, and in his only appearance at that level he scored twice in a 3–0 victory.

In May 1975, at the end of his first full season at Maine Road, Tueart was selected for England in a European Championship qualifier against Cyprus in Limassol. Tueart went on to win six full caps, scoring twice for his country.

He was City's leading scorer in 1975/76 with fourteen League goals, also finding the net eight times in the club's run to Wembley in the League Cup. Tueart clinched a 2–1 victory against Newcastle United with a spectacular overhead kick, a goal that has been played and replayed endlessly on television. In 1976/77 he scored eighteen goals as City were just beaten to the League Championship by a point by Liverpool.

In February 1978, Tueart was lured to America, signing for New York Cosmos for £250,000. However, he returned to Maine Road in 1980 and, though no longer a first-team regular, collected an FA Cup runners-up medal against Spurs in 1981. He left Manchester City in the summer of 1983 and, after a brief spell with Stoke

City, joined Burnley. After an injury-hit season at Turf Moor, he appeared briefly with Irish League club Derry City before retiring.

Dennis Tueart now runs his own corporate promotions company in Manchester, and as a director of his beloved Manchester City can regularly be seen at Maine Road where he leases an executive box.

## LEAGUE RECORD

|  | A | G |
|---|---|---|
| Notts County | 47 (3) | 2 |
| Rotherham United | 121 | 19 |
| Sunderland | 177 | 27 |
| Manchester City | 146 | 4 |
| Southampton | 73 | 7 |
| Stoke City | 59 | 5 |
| Derby County | 34 | 1 |

## HONOURS
FA Cup 1972/73
League Cup 1975/76
65 England caps

# DAVE WATSON
## Central Defender
### Born 5.10.46, Stapleford

A cornerstone of the England sides of the 1970s, DAVE WATSON began his Football League career with Notts County, but most of his games for the Meadow Lane club were at centre-forward. It was only after he had moved to Rotherham United that the Millers' manager Tommy Docherty switched him to centre-half.

One of the best headers of a ball, he joined Sunderland in December 1970, the first of a number of big-money transfers.

He made his international debut in 1974, by which time he had established himself as one of the best centre-halfs outside the top flight. Watson, who had won an FA Cup winners' medal in 1973 as Sunderland beat Leeds United 1–0, was a big-hearted player, always seeming to have the strength to keep his balance and retain possession of the ball. He became an essential part of Ron Greenwood's England side and went on to win sixty-five caps, Greenwood keeping him in the squad until the 1982 World Cup Finals, by which time Watson was thirty-five.

Dave Watson had joined Manchester City in June 1975 and ended his first campaign at Maine Road with a League Cup winners' medal. In 1976/77 he helped City to runners-up spot in the First Division, just a point adrift of League Champions Liverpool.

Watson, who was a virtual ever-present in his four seasons at Maine Road, played briefly for German club Werder Bremen before returning to League action with Southampton, whom he joined in October 1979 for a fee of £200,000. After two and a half seasons at the Dell, Watson moved to Stoke City, where he enjoyed an Indian summer.

He was released to go on an 'illegal' tour of South Africa, which never happened in the end, but finally moved to Vancouver Whitecaps in the NASL. On his return he linked up with Derby County, later playing for Fort Lauderdale Sun, Notts County (again) and non-League Kettering Town.

Watson is now back in the Midlands, living just outside Nottingham at West Bridgford, where he runs a marketing business, Dave Watson International.

# DAVID WEBB
Defender
Born 9.4.46, Stratford

**LEAGUE RECORD**

|  | A | G |
|---|---|---|
| Leyton Orient | 62 | 3 |
| Southampton | 75 | 2 |
| Chelsea | 230 | 21 |
| Queens Park Rangers | 116 | 7 |
| Leicester City | 32 (1) | 0 |
| Derby County | 25 (1) | 1 |
| Bournemouth | 11 | 0 |
| Torquay United | 2 | 1 |

**HONOURS**
FA Cup 1969/70
European Cup Winners Cup
  1970/71

One of Chelsea' most popular players, DAVID WEBB arrived at Stamford Bridge from Southampton in February 1968 in a deal which took Joe Kirkup to the Dell in part exchange. He had played at right-back for the south coast-club but Dave Sexton, who had been his manager at Leyton Orient where he started his league career, initially employed him at centre-half.

Webb distinguished himself with a swashbuckling hat-trick at Ipswich Town on Boxing Day 1968, but when John Dempsey arrived shortly afterwards, he was handed the number 2 shirt that had been vacated by Kirkup.

The rugged defender lacked the pace and agility to make a complete success of the role and his limitations were brutally exposed in the 1970 FA Cup Final at Wembley, when Leeds United's left-winger Eddie Gray tormented him with a display of wizardry. Dave bore his ordeal as Chelsea fans had come to expect of him, making a crucial clearance in extra time; then, and in the replay at Old Trafford, had his revenge. Moving to the centre of defence alongside Dempsey, he crowned a great performance with the winning goal, bundled in at the far post from Ian Hutchinson's long throw.

He continued to partner Dempsey at the heart of the Chelsea defence and his outstanding displays in both matches against Real Madrid in Athens provided ample confirmation of his growing stature. His willingness to do whatever was asked of him in the Chelsea cause (he made occasional emergency appearances as a striker) was never seen more clearly than on Boxing Day 1971, when, with three keepers injured, he took over in goal and kept a clean sheet in the match against Ipswich.

But Webb, who had scored thirty-three goals in 298 games for the Blues, became unsettled in the wake of the disharmony that followed the departure of Hudson and Osgood and joined Queens Park Rangers. Partnering Frank McLintock, Rangers came within a whisker of Championship success, before he had spells with Leicester City and Derby County – both of which ended in relegation!

Appointed player-manager of Bournemouth, he helped the Cherries win promotion to the Third Division before his final appearances as a player came with Torquay United.

David Webb (right) is shown here in his Chelsea days getting the ball past
Brian Dear (West Ham).

He then managed Southend United, taking the Shrimps from the Fourth to the
Second Division in successive seasons in the early '90s, before taking charge of
both Chelsea and Brentford, whom he led to the 1995 play-off qualifiers. On
leaving Griffin Park, Webb managed Southend United for a second time before
having a spell in charge of then non-League Yeovil Town.

# TREVOR WHYMARK

Forward
Born 4.5.50, Diss

**LEAGUE RECORD**

|  | A | G |
| --- | --- | --- |
| Ipswich Town | 249 (12) | 75 |
| Derby County | 2 | 0 |
| Grimsby Town | 83 (10) | 16 |
| Southend United | 37 (2) | 6 |
| Peterborough Utd | 3 | 0 |
| Colchester United | 2 | 0 |

**HONOURS**
FA Cup 1977/78
Second Division Champions 1967/68
Texaco Cup 1972/73
1 England cap

After scoring sixty-five goals for Ipswich Town's youth and reserve teams in 1968/69, TREVOR WHYMARK was given his first-team debut the following season in a 1–0 defeat at Manchester City.

However, it was another three seasons before he established himself as a first-team regular, ending the 1972/73 campaign with eleven goals. Also that season he netted five goals in the Texaco Cup, including one in the second leg of the final against local rivals Norwich City. In 1973/74 he again scored eleven League goals, and in the UEFA Cup second-round first-leg match against Lazio he scored all the club's goals in a 4–0 win. He was joint top scorer in 1974/75, as Town finished third in Division One, before becoming the club's leading scorer for the first time the following season.

Whymark was the club's top scorer again in 1976/77 with more than half his total of thirteen league goals coming in just two games. He scored four in the 7–0 demolition of West Bromwich Albion – the first time an Ipswich player had scored four goals in a First Division match – and then a hat-trick in a 5–0 win over Norwich City in the East Anglian derby.

In 1977/78 Whymark scored four goals in a match for the third time, as Swedish side Landskrona Bois were beaten 5–0. That performance led to him winning his first full cap for England, when he came on as substitute for Terry McDermott in a 2–0 win in Luxembourg. Sadly, Whymark damaged his knee ligaments in a Boxing Day match at Norwich and though he played a few games the following season, he was allowed to leave the club and join Vancouver Whitecaps, after scoring 104 goals in 335 games.

He later played two games for Derby County before Grimsby Town broke their transfer record to sign him. After scoring sixteen goals in ninety-three league games for the Mariners, Whymark ended his League career with spells at Southend United, Peterborough and Colchester United.

On leaving the game, he coached youngsters and ran courses at holiday camps for a number of years before working as a van salesman. Nowadays he coaches part-time at Ipswich Town's academy.

# RAY WILKINS

Midfielder
Born 14.9.56, Hillingdon

**LEAGUE RECORD**

|  | A | G |
| --- | --- | --- |
| Chelsea | 176 (3) | 30 |
| Manchester United | 158 (2) | 7 |
| Queens Park Rangers | 169 (6) | 7 |
| Crystal Palace | 1 | 0 |
| Wycombe Wanderers | 1 | 0 |
| Millwall | 3 | 0 |
| Leyton Orient | 3 | 0 |

**HONOURS**
FA Cup 1982/83
84 England caps

Nicknamed 'Butch' by his father, a former Brentford professional, RAY WILKINS began his career with Chelsea. Captain of the England youth team, he was just eighteen years old when Chelsea manager Eddie McCreadie made him club captain – and, a born leader, he handled the pressure with remarkable assurance and seemed to feel no embarrassment at chivvying or encouraging men ten years his senior.

In 1976/77 he skippered Chelsea to promotion to the First Division – playing just behind the strikers he had the freedom to exploit his creativity to the full. Stylish and assured, he produced a series of imperious displays illuminated by his remarkable awareness and pinpoint forty-yard passes. However, with Chelsea struggling in the lower reaches of the top flight, transfer speculation began to fill the back pages and when the Blues were relegated in 1979, Wilkins rejoined Dave Sexton at Old Trafford, Manchester United paying £875,000 for his signature.

He took a while to settle at Old Trafford but eventually succeeded Martin Buchan as captain. He later captained England but lost both jobs to Bryan Robson. With United he came close to winning the League Championship in his first season but he did win an FA Cup winners' medal in 1983.

In 1984 he joined the exodus to Italy, signing for AC Milan for £1.5 million. After three years he lost his place and moved to French club Paris St Germain. However, Wilkins hardly got a game in the French team and was rescued by Graeme Souness, who signed him for Glasgow Rangers in 1987.

He missed barely a game in two years at Ibrox, winning Scottish League Championship and Skol Cup winners' medals. In November 1989 he returned to London to play for Queens Park Rangers, where he was not to miss a game in his first two seasons at the club.

Awarded an OBE in that year's honours list, he later left Loftus Road to join Crystal Palace. He made only one appearance for the Eagles, however, before he broke a foot.

Awarded an MBE in 1994, he rejoined Queens Park Rangers as player-manager, a position he held for two years. Then, after just eight games of the 1997/98 season, Fulham manager Micky Adams was dismissed and, amid much publicity,

Kevin Keegan arrived with Ray Wilkins as team manager. Fulham made the play-offs despite losing their last three games, but that final spell of poor form cost Wilkins his job. He then returned to Stamford Bridge as Chelsea coach before following Gianluca Vialli to Watford as the Hornets' first-team coach.

# FRANK WORTHINGTON

Forward
Born 23.11.48, Halifax

## LEAGUE RECORD

| | A | G |
|---|---|---|
| Huddersfield Town | 166 (5) | 41 |
| Leicester City | 209 (1) | 72 |
| Bolton Wanderers | 81 (3) | 35 |
| Birmingham City | 71 (4) | 29 |
| Leeds United | 32 | 14 |
| Sunderland | 18 (1) | 2 |
| Southampton | 34 | 4 |
| Brighton & Hove Albion | 27 (4) | 7 |
| Tranmere Rovers | 51 (8) | 21 |
| Preston North End | 10 (13) | 3 |
| Stockport County | 18 (1) | 6 |

## HONOURS

Second Division Champions 1969/70,
  1977/78
8 England caps

From a footballing family – older brothers Bob and Dave, both full-backs, had long League careers – FRANK WORTHINGTON started his career with Huddersfield Town, helping them win the Second Division Championship in 1969/70.

At the end of the 1971/72 season, however, Huddersfield finished bottom of the First Division and the chance came for him to join Liverpool. A fee of £150,000 had been agreed and Worthington duly arrived at Anfield to sign. As a Liverpool player he was subject to a medical examination and the club doctor revealed that Frank had high blood pressure – he had failed the medical.

Leicester City seized their chance and a cut-price Worthington moved on for £80,000. In 1974, Worthington's elegantly effective centre-forward play was rewarded with an England call-up from Sir Alf Ramsey. He held his place under caretaker manager Joe Mercer and went on to make eight appearances. Frank was at that time a true international-class player and should have made many more appearances for his country.

When his old Huddersfield boss Ian Greaves was searching for that extra quality to lift Bolton Wanderers into the First Division, after two agonising near-misses, Worthington went to Bolton on loan in September 1977, and shortly afterwards signed on a permanent basis for a fee of £90,000.

He soon rediscovered the style which had made him one of the best strikers in the game – the ice-cool finishing, the keen positional sense, the close control in tight spots and the neat headed flick-ons. Frank and his co-striker Neil Whatmore banged in thirty goals between them as the Wanderers won the Second Division Championship in 1977/78. The following season Worthington proved his class as both a target man and a finisher. Although Bolton struggled against relegation, Frank ended the season with twenty-four League goals to top the First Division goal-scoring charts. Bolton did the double over Manchester United with Frank hitting two goals in each match – the second in injury time at Old Trafford took him past his career-best total for a season.

And his televised goal against Ipswich Town that season won the 'Goal of the Season' competition.

In October 1980, after a summer playing for Philadelphia Furies in the NASL, he joined Birmingham City for £150,000. He top-scored there and helped them win promotion before moves to Leeds United and Sunderland. The First Division welcomed him back with Southampton before spells with Brighton, Tranmere, Preston and Stockport County.

One of the game's most gifted and colourful strikers, he was approaching his fortieth birthday when he left the first-class game. Since his biography *One Hump or Two?* has been published, Frank now utilises his larger-than-life character to entertain as an after-dinner speaker.

# TERRY YORATH

Midfielder
Born 27.3.50, Cardiff

**LEAGUE RECORD**

|  | A | G |
| --- | --- | --- |
| Leeds United | 120 (21) | 10 |
| Coventry City | 99 | 3 |
| Tottenham Hotspur | 44 (4) | 1 |
| Bradford City | 22 (5) | 0 |
| Swansea City | 1 | 0 |

**HONOURS**
League Champions 1973/74
59 Wales caps

At school TERRY YORATH was good at Rugby, but one day his brother's soccer team was a player short and Terry stepped in. From this accidental beginning Terry went on to win four Welsh schoolboy caps, and eventually signed for Leeds United. He had only played in one League game when, in 1969, he made his full international debut for Wales against Italy.

Yorath was an aggressive, hard-tackling competitor, and a fine clubman. A substitute in Leeds' 1973 FA Cup Final team, he made the starting line-ups for the 1973 European Cup Winners' Cup and 1975 European Cup Finals but only picked up losers' medals. During the club's League Championship-winning season of 1973/74, Yorath played in twenty-eight games and occupied five different positions. Towards the end of his time at Elland Road, Yorath was United's first-team captain, but in August 1976, after scoring 12 goals in 196 League and Cup games, he left Leeds to join Coventry City for a fee of £125,000.

At Highfield Road, Yorath was immediately appointed captain and in his first season with the club did much to steer the Sky Blues clear of relegation. In 1977/78 he partnered Barry Powell when City played a 4–2–4 formation and though they were often outnumbered, they dominated midfield in one of Coventry's best top-flight sides.

However, Yorath moved again in the next season, joining Tottenham Hotspur for £275,000. Signed to add a bit of steel to a midfield that boasted the talents of Hoddle, Ardilles and Villa, Yorath performed the task admirably for a season before being plagued by injuries.

After a spell with Vancouver Whitecaps, he was appointed assistant manager to Trevor Cherry at Bradford City, helping them win the 1984/85 Third Division Championship. He then managed Swansea, leading the Swans to promotion to the Third Division in 1987/88 but he left in February 1989 to become Bradford City's new manager. Things didn't work out and he returned to his old job at Swansea.

Shortly afterwards he became full-time manager of Wales; but although they almost qualified for the 1992 European Championships, his contract was not renewed. He went to Beirut as Lebanese national team coach, and then back to Bradford City before becoming manager of Sheffield Wednesday, from whom he parted company midway through the 2002/03 season.

# The Managers

# BRIAN CLOUGH

One of nine children, Brian Clough worked as a clerk with ICI before joining Middlesbrough. He was one of the club's greatest marksmen with 204 goals in 222 appearances, before moving to Sunderland in July 1961 for a fee of £45,000.

Clough was the leading scorer in the Second Division for three successive seasons and scored forty goals or more every season from 1956 to 1960. He scored sixty-three goals in seventy-four appearances for Sunderland before an injury against Bury on Boxing Day 1962 virtually ended his playing career.

After a spell on Sunderland's coaching staff he took his first steps in management with Hartlepool United, where a friend from his playing days at Middlesbrough, Peter Taylor, joined him. He turned the club's fortunes around, building a squad that was to gain promotion at the end of the 1967/68 season. But by then Clough and Taylor had moved to Derby County, who were then a modest Second Division club. They made a number of major signings – Roy McFarland, Archie Gemmill, Colin Todd, David Nish and John O'Hare – and were soon crowned champions of the Second Division.

In 1971/72, the Rams won the League Championship for the first time in their history and the following season reached the semi-finals of the European Cup before losing to Juventus. In October 1973 Clough shocked the football world by resigning as Derby manager, and the following month he and Taylor accepted an offer to manage Third Division Brighton and Hove Albion.

His stay on the south coast was brief and the following summer he took over at Leeds United as Don Revie's replacement. He was soon making major changes and there were rumours of an unhappy dressing-room atmosphere. The press blamed 'player power' when Clough was sacked after only forty-four days in charge.

He was not out of work for long, though, being appointed manager of Nottingham Forest in January 1975. Over the next eighteen years he was to produce some golden moments for the Reds, including a League Championship, four League Cup wins and two European Cup successes.

Forest won promotion to the First Division in 1977 and a year later clinched the League title. In 1979 they won the European Cup as a Trevor Francis goal was enough to beat Malmo. A year later they confounded the critics when they won the European Cup for a second time. The Reds also played in six League Cup Finals between 1978 and 1992, winning four of them. He did not have too much success in the FA Cup, however, until 1991 when they reached the final, only to lose to Spurs.

Brian Clough was never offered the England job as his views were far too outspoken for the FA. He was offered the Welsh national team manager's job but Forest would not release him to carry out his duties on a part-time basis.

There is no doubt that Brian Clough was one of the greatest managers of all time. He retired in May 1993 amidst a lot of bad publicity, having won just about everything there is to win.

# GORDON LEE

Gordon Lee began his footballing career playing 142 games for Aston Villa, and appeared in the 1961 and 1963 Football League Cup Finals. His first coaching position was with Shrewsbury Town, and he began to gain a reputation as a successful manager when he went to Port Vale, leading them to promotion from the Fourth Division in 1969/70 at his first attempt.

After being appointed manager of Blackburn Rovers and taking them to the Third Division Championship in 1974/75, he became involved in a battle between Blackburn and Newcastle United for his services, and eventually Rovers were forced to let him go.

Rated the best young manager outside the top flight, Lee fashioned the Magpies into a hard-working professional combination, to the joy of Newcastle supporters. He could develop and motivate, yet never seemed to find a place for flair and artistry in his team. Newcastle reached the League Cup final during 1975/76 and mounted a good challenge for both the FA Cup and a European place, but Lee's position was weakened by the loss of Malcolm Macdonald to Arsenal.

In February 1977, Lee was appointed manager of Everton. Though they were into the League Cup semi-finals, Everton were at the bottom of the First Division. By the end of the season, they had risen to ninth place, reached the semi-final of the FA Cup and lost the League Cup Final to Aston Villa but only after two replays. Lee built a side of considerable ability, which finished third in his first full season and were the First Division's highest scorers. During 1977/78, the Blues went 19 games without defeat and finished fourth. Midway through the season, however, Lee was charged with bringing the game into disrepute after criticising a referee for allowing a game to go ahead on a treacherous pitch at the Dell, though an FA disciplinary committee later cleared him.

Lee's forays into the transfer market failed to prevent a miserable slump and he was dismissed in 1981. He managed Preston North End from 1981 to 1983, then coached abroad in climes as disparate as those of Saudi Arabia and Iceland.

In 1988 he became David Pleat's coach at Leicester City and in March 1991 was named as caretaker-boss, helping the club retain their Second Division status before being replaced by Brian Little. On leaving Leicester he stated with dignity that he'd never had to apply for a job in football in his life and wasn't about to start.

# JOHN LYALL

John Lyall was the longest-serving manager in the Football League when he was dismissed by West Ham United in May 1989. Born in Ilford, Lyall played for England Youth against Luxembourg at Upton Park in 1957 and was a member of the West Ham side beaten by Manchester United in the FA Youth Cup Final later that year. He made his League debut for the Hammers against Chelsea in February 1960 but subsequently battled against injuries for three years. He finally conceded defeat, playing his last game for the club at home to Blackburn Rovers in May 1963.

He then worked in the offices at Upton Park for a while before taking up coaching at the club. In 1971 he became assistant manager to Ron Greenwood and then team manager, with Greenwood as general manager, in August 1974. Lyall was then given full managerial responsibilities when Greenwood became England's manager in 1977. During Lyall's management, the Hammers won the FA Cup twice. In 1975 they beat Fulham 2–0 in the final and in 1980 they beat Arsenal 1–0. West Ham also reached the European Cup Winners' Cup Final where they lost 4–2 to Anderlecht in the Heysel Stadium. The club were relegated in 1978 but in 1980/81 they won the Second Division Championship and reached the League Cup Final. The Hammers were relegated again in 1988/89 and Lyall was sacked – despite the club reaching the semi-finals of the League Cup and the sixth round of the FA Cup.

After working as technical co-ordinator with Tottenham Hotspur, he was appointed manager of Ipswich Town. He quickly rebuilt the team and they won the Second Division title in 1991/92. He remained in charge of team affairs at Portman Road until December 1994, when he moved upstairs to become the club's general manager.

# LAWRIE McMENEMY

Lawrie McMenemy failed to make the grade at Newcastle United and joined his local club Gateshead; but in 1961 an injury ended his playing career and he became trainer-coach at the club for the next three years. In 1964 he was appointed manager of non-League Bishop Auckland and transformed them into Northern Premier League champions.

After two years as coach to Sheffield Wednesday, he was appointed manager of Doncaster Rovers, and in his first season with the Yorkshire club he took them to the Championship of the Fourth Division. However, when the Belle Vue club was relegated in 1971, McMenemy was sacked.

A week later he was appointed manager of Grimsby Town and again, at the end of his first season in charge, they too won the Fourth Division Championship. With 63 points, they were three ahead of runners-up Southend United.

In the summer of 1973, McMenemy accepted an offer to become Ted Bates's assistant manager at the Dell, and six months later he was appointed as the club's full-time manager when Bates, the Football League's longest-serving manager, retired to become a director of the club.

At the end of that season, the Saints were relegated, and McMenemy came in for a lot of criticism when they did not bounce straight back – but he did take the club to a shock FA Cup Final victory in 1976, when a Bobby Stokes goal helped them beat Manchester United. McMenemy signed a number of experienced professionals and in 1977/78 the Saints won promotion to the First Division, and a year later they reached the League Cup Final where they lost 3–2 to Nottingham Forest.

In 1983/84 the Saints enjoyed their best ever season in the top flight when they finished runners-up to Liverpool whom they beat 2-0 at home and drew 1-1 at Anfield.

In June 1985 McMenemy moved to Sunderland, but he had a tough time at Roker Park and just under two years later was sacked. After three years out of the game, McMenemy returned as assistant manager to England boss Graham Taylor. More recently he was assistant manager to Northern Ireland team boss Sammy McIlroy, but is now heavily involved with media work.

# BERTIE MEE

Bertie Mee was Arsenal's physiotherapist and little known outside Highbury when he was appointed the Gunners' manager in 1966. As a player, he had a spell as a winger on the books of Derby County before the war, but he did not play in the first team before joining Mansfield Town just before the outbreak of hostilities. He made some guest appearances for Southampton during the war and also appeared in a representative Army Wanderers side in the Middle East.

Forced to retire through injury at the age of twenty-seven, he then spent six years as a sergeant in the RAMC and another twelve as a rehabilitation officer for disabled servicemen. Then, in August 1960, he joined Arsenal as the club's trainer and physiotherapist, replacing Billy Milne who had retired.

A coaching badge and physiotherapy qualifications hardly seemed enough for the challenge of managing Arsenal when he was finally appointed to succeed Billy Wright. However, although Mee was not given to excessive enthusiasm, his ability to communicate his own passion for order and excellence was to revive Arsenal. Also, the team was far more important than any individual, and Mee steered away from the media.

Soon after taking control, Mee was in action on the transfer market, bringing George Graham and Bob McNab to Highbury. In 1967/68 Arsenal lost to Leeds United in the League Cup Final to a controversial goal, and in the following season they reached the final again, only to lose to Third Division Swindon Town. In April 1970, the Gunners won their first major trophy for seventeen years, when they beat Anderlecht 4–3 on aggregate in the final of the Inter Cities Fairs Cup.

The following season was the greatest in Arsenal's history, when Bertie Mee guided the Gunners to a League and FA Cup double. Not surprisingly, he was voted Manager of the Year. Arsenal clinched the League title at White Hart Lane on the Monday before the Cup Final, then went out and beat Liverpool thanks to a great goal by Charlie George.

In 1972 Arsenal reached the Cup Final again but lost to Leeds, and in 1972/73 they were runners-up in the First Division. After this the pressure began to tell and, after a couple of mediocre seasons, Mee announced his retirement in March 1976, remaining in post until Terry Neill took over. He left Highbury in the summer and after a short break from football became a director at Watford.

In short, Bertie Mee was the man who had made Arsenal great again.

# BOB PAISLEY

One of the most successful managers in the history of English soccer, Bob Paisley continued the great work done by his predecessor at Anfield, Bill Shankly, in maintaining Liverpool as one of the great club sides in the world.

Under Paisley, the Reds won many honours including six League Championships, three European Cup victories, three League Cup successes and a UEFA Cup victory. Paisley was voted Manager of the Year a record six times.

As a player, Paisley joined Liverpool from Bishop Auckland, developing into a gritty, tenacious wing-half. He helped Liverpool win the League Championship in 1946/47 and scored the goal that brought the Reds victory over Everton in the 1950 FA Cup semi-final – but much to his disappointment he was left out of the Wembley side.

On hanging up his boots, he joined the Anfield back-room staff and worked his way through the ranks. Starting as assistant trainer he became chief trainer in 1957 and was assistant manager to Bill Shankly for many years before being appointed manager in July 1974.

Paisley had a deep understanding of football and his first master-stroke was to convert Ray Kennedy from striker to an invaluable midfield player. In 1977 he signed Kenny Dalglish to replace Kevin Keegan, and later Graeme Souness – both men who were later to manage the club!

In 1975/76 Liverpool won the League title and the UEFA Cup, beating Bruges 4–3 on aggregate in the final. They retained the Championship in 1976/77 but narrowly missed out on the double when they lost 2–1 to Manchester United – although four days later they beat Borussia Moenchengladbach 3–1 in the final of the European Cup. In 1977/78 they lifted the European Cup again and the following season they won the League Championship with a record sixty-eight points.

Liverpool also took the League title in 1979/80, 1981/82 and 1982/83 and the European Cup for a third time in 1981, beating Real Madrid 1–0. The Reds also appeared in four League Cup Finals under Paisley, winning in 1981, 1982 and 1983.

In June 1983 Paisley decided to retire, but remained at the club as an advisor to his successors Joe Fagan and Kenny Dalglish, and also served on the board of directors.

Paisley had served Liverpool for forty-four years as player, trainer and manager by the time he retired from the board of directors due to ill health in February 1992.

# SIR BOBBY ROBSON

One of the game's most successful managers, Bobby Robson began his career as an amateur with Middlesbrough, but was playing for another local side, Langley Park Juniors, when Fulham manager Bill Dodgin pipped Newcastle United for his signature. In May 1950 Robson duly left his coalmining job to move to London and soon established himself at inside-right alongside Jezzard and Haynes.

Then, in March 1956, Vic Buckingham signed him for West Bromwich Albion for a fee of £25,000, and in seven years at the Hawthorns he scored 61 goals in 240 League games. Also during this time, he was converted to wing-half, renewing his partnership with Johnny Haynes when he won the the first of twenty full caps for England against France in 1958.

Like Haynes, he lost his international place after the 1962 World Cup but then linked up again with the Fulham maestro when he returned to Craven Cottage for a second spell in August 1962. After five more seasons with the Cottagers he moved to North America to manage Vancouver Royals, but in January 1968 he returned to Craven Cottage for a third spell, this time as manager.

Sacked after ten months for failing to arrest the club's decline, he briefly scouted for Chelsea before in January 1969 being appointed manager of Ipswich town.

The first few years in charge proved tough but he began to put together a useful side. The club finished fourth in Division One in both 1972/73 and 1973/74 seasons. They also finished third in the seasons 1974/75, 1976/77 and 1979/80 and were runners-up in 1980/81 and 1981/82. The club also won the UEFA Cup in 1980/81, but Robson's greatest triumph came in the 1978 FA Cup Final, when Ipswich beat Arsenal 1–0.

In July 1982 Robson, who had managed the England 'B' side since 1978, replaced Ron Greenwood as England manager. Although England failed to qualify for the European Championships in 1984, they qualified for the World Cup Finals two years later but lost 2–1 to Argentina in the quarter-finals. After then qualifying with ease for the 1988 European Championships, England lost all of their games in the finals. In 1990 Robson then took England to the World Cup semi-finals, where they were unfortunate to lose to West Germany on penalties after a 1–1 draw.

In August 1990 Robson had had enough of the limelight as England's manager and took over at PSV Eindhoven. They won the Dutch title in both 1990/91 and 1991/92 but failed to find success in Europe. Robson later managed Sporting Lisbon and Barcelona before taking charge of Newcastle United in September 1999.

# RON SAUNDERS

A bustling all-action centre-forward, Ron Saunders made his Football League debut for Everton in 1951, but after only three appearances he moved to non-League Tonbridge. His League career was resurrected by Gillingham, who signed him in May 1957. Then Portsmouth saw his potential, and he went on to make 258 League and Cup appearances for Pompey, scoring 156 goals before later playing for Watford and Charlton Athletic.

Saunders started on the road to management with then Southern League Yeovil Town in 1968, but after less than twelve months he joined Oxford United.

Obviously impressed by his work at the Manor Ground, Norwich City then offered him their vacant manager's post in 1969.

After taking the Canaries to the Second Division Championship in 1971/72 and to the final of the League Cup, he resigned after a poor start to the 1973/74 season. He then had five months in charge at Manchester City before joining Aston Villa in the summer of 1974.

In his first season in charge, Saunders transformed a rather disappointing Villa side into League Cup winners and runners-up in the Second Division, and was named Manager of the Year. Then, in 1980/81, Villa won their first League Championship since 1910. This was an outstanding achievement by Saunders and qualified the club for the following season's European Cup – in which they had reached the quarter-finals when Saunders surprisingly resigned to become manager of Birmingham City.

Here he helped the Blues win promotion from the Second Division in 1985 before joining West Bromwich Albion as manager in February 1986. But here he failed to prevent the Baggies from being relegated, and was sacked in September 1987. When he left the Hawthorns he had completed thirty-six years connected with professional football, in a career that had encompassed eleven League clubs. Although now officially retired, he still acts as an advisor and scout for a number of clubs.

# BOB STOKOE

**B**ob Stokoe played his first game for Newcastle United on Christmas Day 1950 as centre-forward against Middlesbrough – and scored a goal! After switching to centre-half he became a regular in the Magpies' side and went on to appear in 287 games for the club, gaining an FA Cup winners' medal in 1955 as United beat Manchester City 3–1. Then, in December 1961, after fourteen years on the St James Park staff, Stokoe was appointed player-manager of Bury.

Stokoe resigned from the Gigg Lane club in the summer of 1965 and took over at struggling Charlton Athletic. After selling two of the club's most popular players in Mike Bailey and Billy Bonds, Stokoe was sacked in September 1967, but was paid compensation by the club after he had left.

The following month he was appointed manager of Rochdale, but after helping the Lancashire club avoid re-election for the third season running he resigned and took over at Carlisle United. After taking the Cumbrian side to the semi-finals of the League Cup, Stokoe left to become manager of Blackpool in December 1970. Though the Seasiders won the Anglo-Italian Trophy, he couldn't get the club back into the top flight and in November 1972 he accepted an offer to manage Sunderland.

It was a great move for him, for at the end of his first season the Roker Park club beat Leeds United 1–0 in the FA Cup Final at Wembley. Few will forget Stokoe charging across the pitch to hug Jim Montgomery at the final whistle, the keeper having made some memorable saves. Sunderland then entered European competition for the first time but went out to Sporting Lisbon in the second round of the Cup Winners' Cup.

The Sunderland manager was by now busy in the transfer market, bringing Dave Watson, Dennis Tueart and Tony Towers to Roker Park, and in 1975/76 he led the club back to the top flight as Second Division Champions. Sadly, though, it all went wrong for him the following season and he resigned.

A year later he returned for his second spell as manager of Bury but they struggled in the lower reaches of the Third Division and he resigned. He had another stint in charge of Blackpool and then again with Rochdale but they finished ninety-second in the Football League and he left. Another of his former clubs, Carlisle United, then appointed him manager again and in 1981/82 he took them back to the Second Division as runners-up.

Stokoe later resigned his post and had a spell as caretaker manager of Sunderland in 1986/87. He then acted as a scout for both Chelsea and Swindon before being a consultant at Bury, but in 1996 he returned to the north-east to live in Hexham.

# TONY WADDINGTON

One of the most respected managers in the game, Tony Waddington gained a reputation for giving ageing stars who were nearing the end of their careers an 'Indian Summer'. He was at the Victoria Ground for twenty-five years as third-team coach, assistant manager and manager, holding the manager's job for seventeen years. For most of his time in charge, Stoke were a consistent First Division club and they also won their first major trophy in 1972, when they beat Chelsea in the League Cup Final at Wembley.

Waddington started his playing career at Manchester United as an amateur in 1941, while serving in the Royal Navy. Playing at either full-back or wing-half, he moved to Crewe Alexandra in 1946, but six years later he was forced to retire from the game through a knee injury.

He arrived at Stoke in 1952 as coach and five years later was promoted to assistant manager. In June 1960 he succeeded Frank Taylor as manager and introduced new tactics, a new style of play and several new players to Stoke supporters. In an interesting move, he signed 46-year-old Stanley Matthews from Blackpool to help the team win promotion from the Second Division. Another Waddington master-stroke was the signing of Burnley's Jimmy McIroy for £25,000 in that promotion-winning season of 1962/63. Stoke gained an interesting reputation as a veterans' team as he signed players such as Eddie Clamp, Alex Elder, David Herd, Roy Vernon and Dennis Viollet. He also signed England goalkeeper Gordon Banks.

The Stoke manager also brought the club a reputation for entertaining and successful football. In 1964 the Potters reached the final of the League Cup but lost 4–3 on aggregate to Leicester City. They also reached the semi-finals of the FA Cup in 1971 and 1972, losing to Arsenal on both occasions. His major triumph came in 1972 when the club reached Wembley for the first time. They played in Europe for the first time the following season, but with the departure of most of their leading players in 1976/77, the club were relegated and, in March 1977, Waddington left.

Referred to by many as 'Mr Stoke City', he returned to management two years later with Crewe but in July 1981 he left. He was appointed Associate Director of Stoke City in the summer of 1993, a position he retained until his death the following January.

# Statistics

# Best XI

Selecting a 'best' team can be fascinating but it can also be highly provocative. Below is my best team selected from the hundred players included in this book.

1. Peter Shilton
2. Phil Neal
3. Kevin Beattie
4. Graeme Souness
5. Dave Watson
6. Emlyn Hughes
7. Liam Brady
8. Kevin Keegan
9. Malcolm Macdonald
10. Trevor Brooking
11. Steve Heighway
12. Frank Worthington

# Top Tens

### MOST LEAGUE APPEARANCES

| | | |
|---|---|---|
| 1. | Peter Shilton | 1,005 |
| 2. | Tommy Hutchinson | 795 |
| 3. | Ray Clemence | 758 |
| 4. | Frank Worthington | 757 |
| 5. | Phil Parkes | 743 |
| 6. | Asa Hartford | 742 |
| 7. | Mick Mills | 732 |
| 8. | Steve Perryman | 725 |
| 9. | Mick Channon | 718 |
| 10. | Phil Neal | 706 |

### MOST LEAGUE GOALS

| | | |
|---|---|---|
| 1. | Ted MacDougall | 256 |
| 2. | Frank Worthington | 234 |
| 3. | Mick Channon | 232 |
| 4. | Tony Brown | 229 |
| 5. | Martin Chivers | 220 |
| 6. | Bob Latchford | 218 |
| 7. | Malcolm Macdonald | 191 |
| 8. | Trevor Francis | 176 |
| 9. | Paul Mariner | 175 |
| 10. | John Toshack | 173 |

## MOST LEAGUE APPEARANCES (ONE CLUB)

| | | |
|---|---|---|
| 1. | Steve Perryman (Tottenham Hotspur) | 655 |
| 2. | Tony Brown (West Bromwich Albion) | 574 |
| 3. | Mick Mills (Ipswich Town) | 561 |
| 4. | Frank Lampard (West Ham United) | 551 |
| 5. | Trevor Brooking (West Ham United) | 528 |
| 6. | Mick Channon (Southampton) | 511 |
| 7. | Alistair Robertson (West Bromwich Albion) | 506 |
| 8. | Joe Corrigan (Manchester City) | 476 |
| 9. | Emlyn Hughes (Liverpool) | 474 |
| 10. | Ray Clemence (Liverpool) | 470 |

## MOST GOALS (ONE CLUB)

| | | |
|---|---|---|
| 1. | Tony Brown (West Bromwich Albion) | 218 |
| 2. | Mick Channon (Southampton) | 185 |
| 3. | John Richards (Wolverhampton Wanderers) | 144 |
| 4. | Trevor Francis (Birmingham City) | 119 |
| 5. | Martin Chivers (Tottenham Hotspur) | 118 |
| 6. | Bob Latchford (Everton) | 106 |
| 7. | Ted MacDougall (Bournemouth) | 103 |
| 8. | Joe Royle (Everton) | 102 |
| 9. | Martin Chivers (Southampton) | 97 |
| 10. | Paul Mariner (Ipswich Town) | 96 |
| | Alan Curtis (Swansea City) | 96 |

## MOST INTERNATIONAL APPEARANCES

| | | |
|---|---|---|
| 1. | Peter Shilton (England) | 125 |
| 2. | Ray Wilkins (England) | 84 |
| 3. | Liam Brady (Republic of Ireland) | 72 |
| 4. | Brian Flynn (Wales) | 66 |
| 5. | Dave Watson (England) | 65 |
| 6. | Martin O'Neill (Northern Ireland) | 64 |
| 7. | Kevin Keegan (England) | 63 |
| 8. | Emlyn Hughes (England) | 62 |
| 9. | Ray Clemence (England) | 61 |
| 10. | Terry Yorath (Wales) | 59 |